Overlord – 1944

Bracknell Paper no. 5
A Symposium on the Normandy Landings

25 March 1994

Sponsored jointly by the Royal Air Force Historical Society and the
Royal Air Force Staff College Bracknell

First published in the UK in 1995.

ISBN 0 9519824 3 5

Typesetting and origination by Alan Sutton Publishing Ltd
Printed in Great Britain by Hartnolls, Bodmin, Cornwall.

Royal Air Force Historical Society

Contents

SUPREME HEADQUARTERS

ALLIED EXPEDITIONARY FORCE

Soldiers, Sailors and Airmen of the Allied Expeditionary Force!

You are about to embark upon the Great Crusade, toward which we have striven these many months. The eyes of the world are upon you. The hopes and prayers of liberty-loving people everywhere march with you. In company with our brave Allies and brothers-in-arms on other Fronts, you will bring about the destruction of the German war machine, the elimination of Nazi tyranny over the oppressed peoples of Europe, and security for ourselves in a free world.

Your task will not be an easy one. Your enemy is well trained, well equipped and battle-hardened. He will fight savagely.

But this is the year 1944 ! Much has happened since the Nazi triumphs of 1940-41. The United Nations have inflicted upon the Germans great defeats, in open battle, man-to-man. Our air offensive has seriously reduced their strength in the air and their capacity to wage war on the ground. Our Home Fronts have given us an overwhelming superiority in weapons and munitions of war, and placed at our disposal great reserves of trained fighting men. The tide has turned ! The free men of the world are marching together to Victory !

I have full confidence in your courage, devotion to duty and skill in battle. We will accept nothing less than full Victory !

Good Luck ! And let us all beseech the blessing of Almighty God upon this great and noble undertaking.

Dwight Eisenhower

Preface

The fifth in the World War Two series of Bracknell Symposia, Overlord – 1944, was held at the RAF Staff College on March 25th.

Again sponsored jointly by the RAF Historical Society and the College, Overlord represented a subject of mammoth proportions which had to be boiled down into one day. That it was successfully accomplished is a tribute to the organisers.

The proceedings were chaired by Air Chief Marshal Sir Michael Armitage. The morning session painted in the broad picture and outlined the Command structure. This was followed by lectures on planning and preparation and the campaign itself. Of particular interest was an outline of the Luftwaffe's situation and response – in the face of the largest operational air fleet ever seen.

The discussion groups in the afternoon proved lively and most interesting. In this book are the edited papers and a digest of the work of the discussion groups.

Gratitude is due to Henry Probert, Geoffrey Thorburn, Sebastian Cox and Peter Love, who not only assisted with the transcriptions of the tapes from the discussion groups but also prepared the synopsis which appears in this volume. Thanks go too to Peter Singleton, John Peaty, Christina Goulter and Peter Mason for their help in transcribing. Peter Singleton and the Air Historical Branch have also been most helpful with pictures.

Derek Wood
Editor

1. Welcome by the Commandant

Air Vice-Marshal Donaldson MBE

Good morning ladies and gentlemen. The Staff College offers a sincere welcome to the RAF Historical Society, in particular its President Marshal of the Royal Air Force Sir Michael Beetham and its Chairman Air Marshal Sir Freddie Sowrey, and indeed to the very distinguished group of lords and knights of the realm assembled here today, and all other members of the Historical Society. I attach great importance to the link between the Historical Society and the Advanced Staff Course of the Staff College because the student body are at about that stage in their ageing process where they are willing to look back a little as well as looking forward. They are now able to consider the implications of some of the RAF's historical activities and to look at the lessons they can draw from them; and being able to look back in a symposium such as this adds intellectual vigour to their studies of the past and its lessons. So this is a very important part of their course and that is why I attach such importance to the link with your Society. We are also enjoined these days to look at joint operations more and more in our consideration of military and air power, and to look at the joint perspective. We could not have a more joint operation than the Allied invasion of Europe in 1944. So today's topic is extremely relevant to the studies here at the Staff College.

2. *Introductory Remarks by the Chairman*

Air Chief Marshal Sir Michael Armitage KCB CBE

As your Chairman for this study day I have three tasks: to introduce the distinguished speakers; to draw out the main points emerging from the main talks and the group discussions; and thirdly to keep the programme on schedule.

We are dealing today with the largest and most complex military operation in history, an operation with endless facets of military skills; and we have only four hours in which to do it. In such a short time we cannot hope to give a comprehensive account of the Normandy invasion. Our aim therefore is to bring out the air lessons of an operation which was above all a joint service affair, and our purpose this morning is to stimulate discussions in the seminar groups this afternoon.

The organisers have given much thought to the way we should proceed, and have decided on certain limitations. We shall therefore deal first with the essential background to the campaign, then to the invasion itself, and finally to some of the events up to but not beyond the advance to the River Seine. We are obliged to omit whole areas of possible study, including the intelligence background which contributed so much to our success. We have had to take for granted the vast naval effort so essential in the assault and later on. I apologise to our naval friends for the omission. We confine ourselves almost entirely to the British and the German defenders opposing them. It may seem odd to give little attention to the American and Canadian divisions, and to concentrate on the 106 British squadrons at the expense of the 164 American 9th Air Force squadrons and I crave the indulgence of the American and other Allied colleagues in our audience for these shortcomings. All our forces, however, faced more or less the same challenges during the invasion and afterwards, and the conclusions we reach will be equally applicable to all the other forces engaged.

It is a great pleasure to introduce as our first speaker John Terraine, who is well known to all with an interest in military history, and has graced a number of our previous seminars. He is a prolific author, having written ten books on the First World War, a biography of Lord Mountbatten, *Business in Great Waters*, a study of the U-boat campaigns of both world wars, and *The Right of the Line*, a standard text about the RAF in Europe in the Second World War. He has the unenviable task of setting the whole thing in the context of all that went before, and if anyone can make sense of that huge canvas in 25 minutes it is John Terraine.

3. *Overlord – The Broad Context*

Mr John Terraine FRHistS

Operation OVERLORD: it was well-named: the paramount preoccupation of the Western Allies in the Second World War, the overlord of all their strategy. It was, in the words of Humphrey Wynn and Susan Young (*Prelude to Overlord*), "the largest and most complex single military operation the world had ever seen". It involved just under 7,000 sea-going vessels, 150,000 soldiers and 1,500 tanks to be transported to France in the first 48 hours, 11,590 powered aircraft and 3,500 gliders. It was war on the wide screen – very wide indeed. How did it come about?

The origins of large events usually run deep – this one, I think, can be dated to the disastrous days of 1940, the Allied defeat in the Battle of France and the evacuation of Europe. With the battle still raging, on 6 June (a pregnant date!) 1940, Churchill minuted:

> "I look to the Joint Chiefs of Staff to propose me measures for a vigorous, enterprising and ceaseless offensive against the whole German-occupied coastline."

In the light of what we know now, and what Churchill knew then, the notion of a British "offensive" was bizarre. We would shortly have no effective allies; we would be fighting for our lives in the Battle of Britain, and after that in the Battle of the Atlantic; our loss of equipment in France was virtually catastrophic and our war industries were still being created; all three Services had sustained heavy losses. How could Churchill even think – let alone talk – of a "ceaseless offensive"?

It was more than talk; it immediately became a programme. To begin with, it was a programme of landing-craft construction, which could only be offensive; a study of the techniques of opposed landings, which could only be offensive; combined three-Service training, which could only be offensive. Above all there was Combined Operations Command, of which Lord Louis Mountbatten became Chief in October 1941, with the rank Air Marshal as well as Lieutenant-General and his normal rank of Vice-Admiral. He said that Churchill's brief for his new post was clear and simple:

> "I want you to turn the south coast of England from a bastion of defence into a springboard of attack."

This went far beyond a policy of raids and pinpricks; it spelt a true counter-offensive, but sadly, for the time being, that was still far beyond our means. Yet preparations could begin; the first necessity was a vast quantity of information, and that was already being systematically collected. While the Commandos kept the public happy with their daring raids, a different set of men at Combined Ops HQ was working full-time on a project which must often have had a dreamlike quality in 1941. But very soon the assault on Fortress Europe would become the commanding reality.

It was the Japanese who brought about the transformation. Their attack on Pearl Harbor in December brought America into the war; now Britain had an ally with immense resources, and many things became possible that had only been dreams before. At the ARCADIA Conference in Washington in December 1941 and January 1942, the Americans proclaimed their astonishing decision to set aside their natural instinct to take their revenge on the Japanese, and instead go for "Germany First". It was spelt out by the two Allies that this meant a massive build-up of American air and ground forces in Britain (known as BOLERO) for a direct attack across the Channel, preceded by a mounting bomber offensive against Germany herself. These activities were not alternatives. For complete victory, both were necessary. I regard these agreements as very remarkable achievements in themselves. They meant that from January 1942 the whole thrust of Anglo-American strategy would be towards a decisive campaign in North-West Europe, on the ground and in the air. As I said in T*he Right of the Line*:

> "Henceforth, whatever contributed to this end would promote the prime intention; whatever impeded it would be, to a greater or lesser extent, harmful."

Seen in this light, the name "OVERLORD" seems to me to express very precisely the meaning of the ARCADIA decisions.

Needless to say, the fulfilment of the decisions was rather more difficult than the taking of them. Two resolute enemies bent their energies to preventing it, and 1942 unfolded as a very grim year for the anti-Hitler, anti-Japanese alliance. The route to Normandy in 1944 was not smooth; indeed, there were times when it looked as though the alliance might fall apart before we could get there. Inevitably, there were casualties along the way, which need to be looked at.

Hitler had, in fact, signed his own death-warrant in June 1941 when he launched Operation BARBAROSSA, the invasion of the Soviet Union. It is easy to say that now – it looks totally obvious in the blinding light of hindsight. It didn't look like that in 1942. There were continuous alarms as the German armies performed one encirclement of large Soviet forces after another, and all the indications were that the Soviet Union might collapse at any moment, while in the Far East the rising tide of Japanese conquest tested the resolution of the Allies to its limits.

Very naturally, all through the year the Soviet Government uttered repeated and very emphatic calls for help from the West – not just help in the form of weapons and supplies which Britain and America did their best to provide despite their own shortages, but help in the form which was encapsulated in the slogan "Second Front Now!". To the British Chiefs of Staff, who had been confronting the practicalities of cross-Channel invasion for a long time, it was very obvious in 1942 that the means for such a project just did not exist. On the contrary, they saw clearly that an attempt with what resources they had risked a really serious failure, a disaster which would profit no one except the enemy.

Nevertheless, in extremity, even that had to be contemplated. And so the whole vast operation which was later called OVERLORD was put in jeopardy by a desperate scheme called SLEDGEHAMMER. This was what earlier times would have called a "forlorn hope" – a desperate remedy for a desperate situation: an attempt to mount a sort of super-raid on a larger scale than Dieppe and even form a permanent bridgehead in France for exploitation later, if the Soviet Union seemed to be reaching the point of imminent complete collapse. (There were some optimists who actually suggested that Germany might be reaching such a point, but not many, and the German Army did not encourage their fantasies.)

All one can say is, "Thank God it never came to that"; just thinking about SLEDGEHAMMER makes one shiver. Somehow, the Allies got through the year, and by December 1942 there was light at the end of the tunnel: a decisive victory at last in the Desert War, at El Alamein;

the advance to Tunisia in progress; a successful landing in North Africa – not quite the success that was hoped for, but not a bad beginning for joint British/American enterprises. In the Far East, the Japanese drive was visibly halted. And on the Eastern Front the seemingly unstoppable German advance was also halted – at Stalingrad. Not only were the Germans definitely stopped – the Russians were counter-attacking. It was the turning-point.

The next Allied Conference, in January 1943 at Casablanca, beheld a very different scene from what had faced ARCADIA. It was presented to the world through a screen of beaming faces – it was now de rigueur for the Allied leaders, military as well as civil, always to be seen roaring with laughter. This was not always easy to arrange: General de Gaulle, for example, and Joseph Stalin, did not always respond well to the exhortation, "Smile, please". And at Casablanca, behind the jolly laughter there were serious divergences between the two Western Powers. The Americans became definitely restive, and this was understandable.

When they had said at ARCADIA, "Germany First", what the Americans had meant was "knocking out Germany first" – and fairly soon; they did not mean engaging a very small portion of the German Army on the wrong side of the Mediterranean. They wanted the big attack in north-west Europe, now called ROUNDUP, in 1943. But what they got at Casablanca was HUSKY (the invasion of Sicily), then followed by AVALANCHE (the landing at Salerno) and SHINGLE (Anzio), and what turned into the hard-fought, long-drawn-out Italian campaign. Thanks to some very firm and factually well-supported argument by the British Chiefs of Staff, headed here by General Sir Alan Brooke and Air Chief Marshal Sir Charles Portal, the Americans found themselves committed to a Mediterranean strategy which a good many of them soon translated into a rampant sample of British imperialism. It may be going too far to say that the alliance was threatened with absolute rupture, but there is no doubt that a number of influential Americans came to reflect upon Casablanca with a nasty aftertaste of being "conned". For it became quite clear that one thing that had definitely taken place at Casablanca was the quiet burial of ROUNDUP – without obsequies.

With HUSKY scheduled for July – an unpredictable adventure, being the first of the great amphibious operations by the Allies in the European theatre – and its consequences equally unpredictable but likely to be extensive, there was clearly not going to be a cross-Channel operation in 1943. However, one large step forward was taken with the appointment of a Chief of Staff to the still unnamed Supreme

Allied Commander. He was Lieutenant-General Sir Frederick Morgan, and it was his brainwave to enunciate the thoroughly misleading codename COSSAC for himself and his job – which was nothing less than to guide and coordinate all preparations for the big event in 1944.

The enemy, of course, had their say in these matters. Contrary to all Allied expectations, the Axis forces in North Africa held out until May 1943 – a serious delaying factor. The Allies took a quarter of a million Axis prisoners in Tunisia, about 150,000 of them being German. Coming on top of over 90,000 taken prisoner at Stalingrad in February (though the total Axis loss for that savage battle has been reckoned at 541,000), this victory confirmed the great change in the war: the German Army would never be the same again.

Yet a victory of a quite different kind was also required to release the spring of the Allied offensive in 1944. At the head of the final report of the Combined Chiefs of Staff at Casablanca they stated:

> "The defeat of the U-boat must remain a first charge on the resources of the United Nations."

This was scarcely surprising. Axis submarines, chiefly German, but also Japanese and Italian, had sunk 1,160 ships (over 6¾ million tons of shipping) in 1942, over 1,000 of the ships and nearly 5½ million tons of shipping being lost in the North Atlantic. And there was worse to follow: March 1943 was the worst month of the whole Atlantic battle, with 41 ships lost in the first ten days and 56 in the second ten days – more than half a million tons in just 20 days. The Admiralty itself recorded that

> "the Germans never came so near to disrupting communications between the New World and the Old as in the first 20 days of March 1943."

What this meant to OVERLORD may be judged from the fact that by the end of 1942 the intended massive build-up of American strength in Britain (BOLERO) amounted to less than 100,000 men – a hopeless position.

By the end of May, however, the picture was transformed. Admiral Dönitz had accepted defeat in the Atlantic and virtually removed his U-boat fleet to more congenial areas; as Ronald Lewin said,

> By the autumn of 1943 the Battle of the Atlantic had been reduced to an acceptable running skirmish. There were no more

> disasters. Certainly the path had been cleared for those immense movements of men and supplies without which the next year's return to Europe would have been impossible."

OVERLORD is only to be properly understood in relation to those "immense movements" into north-west Europe which were the sequel to D-Day – 5½ million men, 970,000 vehicles and 18 million tons of supplies. As I said in my last book, there could be

> "no conceivable notion of building up and maintaining such a force with undefeated U-boats at its back."

Thanks to the Atlantic victory, the U-boats proved to be a spent force. The sea-lanes were secured; the BOLERO build-up could be resumed and expanded. Only in one element did the vista look discouraging. Contrary to the hopes and beliefs of the Allied bomber commanders (often referred to as "the bomber barons"), in particular General Carl Spaatz, commanding the United States Strategic Air Forces in Europe, and Air Chief Marshal Sir Arthur Harris, AOC Bomber Command, their Combined Bomber Offensive, with which they fully intended to make OVERLORD unnecessary, had not prospered. Both the United States 8th Army Air Force and Bomber Command found themselves facing unacceptable casualty rates, chiefly inflicted by German fighters. Partly through increased production (despite the bombing of German industry) and partly through stripping other fronts to the bone, the Germans increased their fighter force by over 600 aircraft in 1943, 68% of them in the West. The presence of these fighters, as Webster and Frankland rightly say, "hung like a spectre over all the plans and preparations for OVERLORD".

And then, in December 1943, came the miracle. The North American Aviation Company's P-51B fighter, incorporating the Rolls-Royce Merlin engine, arrived to transform the daylight strategic air offensive. Known as the Mustang, this was a fighter which could escort the bomber stream to Berlin and beyond – "an aircraft with the range of a bomber and the performance of a fighter", truly an aviation miracle. Thanks to the P-51B, the 8th Air Force was able to erode the German fighter force to such an extent in February and March 1944 that thereafter air superiority passed unquestionably to the Allies. As trained night-fighter pilots were increasingly drafted to daytime operations as replacements, Bomber Command profited first from this American victory, with significant results as it carried out the Transportation Plan for isolating the Normandy battlefield. As we shall shortly see, already in the stage of preparation, then on D-Day (June 6) itself, and throughout the OVERLORD campaign, this Allied air supremacy was to be a dominating factor.

What happened on the sixth of June was the opening of the biggest Combined Operation in history, an air, sea and land operation which not only combined the Services concerned, but, by virtue of being also a coalition endeavour, called for the maximum of inter-Allied cooperation. For such an enterprise one could never have too much of that, and it is no secret that there were flaws, which we shall be discussing; it would have been amazing if there had been none, but certainly on D-Day itself inter-Allied disagreements were barely visible. As the campaign developed, one of its most exhilarating features was the warm, productive cooperation of the two Tactical Air Forces (2nd TAF and the 9th US Army Air Force) which provided the ground troops with the close support which, in the light of experiences in the Desert, North Africa, Sicily and Italy, was now considered an essential battle requirement.

This was not only a Western viewpoint; too often overlooked in histories of 1944 is the Eastern Front contribution to the defeat of Germany, Operation BAGRATION, which began just over a fortnight after D-Day, on the third anniversary of Hitler's invasion of the USSR, 22 June. BAGRATION performed the destruction of the German Army Group Centre in the space of the next four weeks, taking out twenty-eight German divisions from the Order of Battle, some 350,000 men, and making a hole 250 miles wide in the German line. For this purpose the Soviets used about 1¾ million men, over 27,000 guns and rocket-launchers, over 4,000 tanks and self-propelled guns – and 5,327 aircraft in close support, plus 700 bombers of their Long Range Force.

East and West we observe the momentous effects of the eclipse of the German Air Force. In Normandy, as OVERLORD proceeded, as I said in *The Right of the Line*, there occurred

> "an outstanding triumph of air power. It was air power that paved the way into Europe; air power covered the landings and made it impossible for the Germans to concentrate against them; air power maintained interdiction, and pressure on the enemy when the 'master plan' failed; air power completed the overwhelming victory."

Chairman

We could not possibly have had a more valuable analytical platform from which to approach the rest of our study day. We are very fortunate to have as our next speaker Field Marshal the Lord Bramall, a most distinguished soldier and one well known to everyone here – not least from his time in Whitehall as CGS, notably during the Falklands campaign. He is himself a noted military historian, and I am sure that most of us have read – better still bought – that excellent book of reference, *The Chiefs* – the story of how the COS structure came about, with some very penetrating analyses of the personalities involved. More directly relevant to today's study, Lord Bramall landed in Normandy on D+1 and he was in action throughout the rest of the campaign in north-west Europe, winning the MC in the process. Lord Bramall's subject is the higher command structure and the commanders.

4. *The Higher Command Structures and Commanders*

Field Marshal the Lord Bramall KG GCB OBE MC JP

In speaking to you about the Command arrangements for Operation OVERLORD I shall start by showing how the outline Command set-up looked on paper; and then explain how it was arrived at and, more importantly, how it worked in practice.

At the top of the structure was SHAEF (Supreme HQ Allied Expeditionary Force) at Bushey Park, with a Supreme Commander and a Deputy Supreme Commander. Below them – at Portsmouth, in London initially, and at Stanmore – were three Cs-in-C for naval, land and air forces, who would work together in all the planning stages, and command or control their respective forces. The land C-in-C (also C-in-C British 21st Army Group, with its US increment) was made responsible for coordinating the whole land battle and commanding the British, Canadian and American armies until the breakout had been achieved and a second (US) Army Group (12th Army Group) could be inserted; at this moment (still then to be determined) both these Army Groups would operate directly under the Supreme Commander.

Then, under their respective Cs-in-C were:

a. two Naval Task Forces, one British and one American, with assault and bombardment forces for each of the five beaches and a follow-up force for each national sector;
b. two assault armies, 2nd British and 1st US, each initially of two Corps;
c. two follow-up armies, 1st Canadian and 3rd US;
d. two Tactical Air Forces, both at Uxbridge, 2nd British and 9th US, to give direct air support to the British and American land forces – together with an RAF airborne/transport force. The Allied Expeditionary Air Forces also had a call on the

independent strategic bomber force of Bomber Command and 8th US Air Force.

All quite straightforward, you might say, so did it work? Well, of course, it did, because the whole operation was ultimately triumphantly successful and even caught up with the original time schedule – but not exactly as smoothly and harmoniously as one might have hoped. This was because, whatever command set-up you had on paper, you were dealing with powerful personalities, all with their own idiosyncrasies, likes and antagonisms; at the height of the war, with past personal experiences influencing their judgement, personal relationships could be quite significant. The result was that, although up to and including D-Day all the planning problems were solved and command decisions taken without too much trouble (although some rather late), within the first week of the landing cracks had begun to appear in the relationships between the air and the ground commanders.

First let me briefly go back to how these appointments came to be made. The top job of Supreme Allied Commander might have become an Allied tug of war, because General Alan Brooke, the Chief of the Imperial General Staff and Chairman of the British Chiefs of Staff, hoped to be given the job, and indeed Winston Churchill said he would back him for it. But the Americans were adamant that there should be an American in overall command. This was partly because, after the British Chiefs' of Staff (quite correct) reluctance to contemplate a landing in north-west Europe in 1942 or even 1943 (preferring to develop the Mediterranean Theatre), they still had some doubts about our enthusiasm for the whole enterprise; and also because, after the initial bridgehead battle, their troops would outnumber the British and Canadians.

General Marshall (the great Chief of the US Army Staff), was at one time considered, but President Roosevelt felt that he could not be spared from Washington. So, with Churchill's eventual agreement, the popular Eisenhower, who had proved himself a good coordinator of diverse Allied factions in North Africa and the Mediterranean, was selected. And although Eisenhower lacked experience of the actual battlefield and of commanding land forces, as a Supreme Commander, capable of taking the big decisions and welding the Allies into a team, he was obviously a good choice. This meant that his deputy should be British and, in view of the great importance of the air plan and the air battle, it logically had to be a British airman, for which the obvious selection (as well as Eisenhower's own preference) was the brilliant, intellectual and sharp Air Chief Marshal Tedder, who had commanded successfully the Allied air forces in the Mediterranean.

The Naval Commander-in-Chief also pretty well chose himself. Admiral Ramsay had got the British Army out of Dunkirk, put the Allies ashore in Sicily and was the Royal Navy's leading expert on large-scale combined operations. Energetic, realistic and innovative, he was just the man to assemble and deploy the great armada of British and American ships, get them across the Channel without enemy interruption and land the forces safely on the other side. All this, with the Air Force's help, he did with conspicuous success and indeed continued to support the land forces very significantly with devastatingly accurate naval bombardment in the crucial bridgehead battle.

For the assault and bridgehead battle itself, the overall land forces commander was clearly crucial. The tactical battle had to be coordinated by one man, working to a master plan, and since the British had both the more experienced battlefield commanders and the greater number of troops in the assault phase, it clearly had to be a "Brit". Eisenhower (and to some extent Churchill, who much admired him) wanted for the job the brave, urbane and laid-back Alexander, because not surprisingly it was thought he would be easier to handle than the abrasive, egoistical and supremely self-confident Bernard Montgomery. But Alexander was not a patch on Montgomery as a strategist and manager of a battlefield; this was fully recognised by Brooke, who persuaded Churchill that Alexander should remain in Italy and that Montgomery should be appointed to OVERLORD and brought back as soon as possible to put his own stamp on the preliminary plans drawn up by the OVERLORD planners under General Freddie Morgan.

What a fortunate decision this was, because I believe that as much as any other single factor the personality, self-confidence and professional leadership of Montgomery contributed to the success of this great and ambitious enterprise which, if it had failed, could have postponed the end of the war indefinitely.

What Monty did was to take a plan that would not have worked, convert it into one on a broader front (two armies up), with more assault divisions and a quicker build-up, and invigorate and give firm direction and grip to a staff which was confused and uncertain. Then by endless morale-boosting visits to military and civilian audiences alike, culminating in the epic briefing to senior OVERLORD commanders at St Paul's School, in front of the King and the Prime Minister, he convinced everyone – commanders, the ordinary soldiers and the country at large – that the "Second Front" was a feasible operation and was going to be triumphantly successful. Churchill had doubts, so did Brooke and Eisenhower, but Monty's self-confidence never faltered. We were going to win, and certainly all of us about to take part in OVERLORD were greatly heartened and inspired by that confidence. It was electric, and leadership of the highest quality. Little did we know what a close run thing it was going to be in certain respects.

At the same time, particularly in his briefing at St Paul's, Monty showed he was a realist. He knew his opponent, Rommel, respected his calibre and realised that, as quickly as possible, Rommel would use his armoured forces to try to drive the embryo bridgeheads into the sea. He appreciated that the fundamental problem was how to bring in forces fast enough over the beaches and through the Mulberry Harbour to be assembled at Arromanches, so as to match the German build-up which would benefit from their interior lines of communication. So not only did he have to have a deception plan to persuade the Germans they could not weaken their 15th Army in the Pas de Calais, but above all there had to be a major air effort, not only to win the air battle and create the right conditions for the landing, but also to interdict the battlefield to prevent German forces arriving there, or at least arriving in any shape to exert their proper effectiveness. In this respect the barriers of the Seine to the east and the Loire to the south were to prove invaluable.

And Monty, despite his later contretemps with some of the air commanders, did understand air power. Indeed he was one of the few senior army officers who did. Monty had already pontificated on changing the Principles of War by adding a new first principle – "First win the air battle". He also realised that the use of air power was not just the army shouting for the support it wanted, when it wanted it, but army and air force commanders sitting side by side and reading the battle together to ensure that the operations on the ground and in the air were looked on as one whole, with the air force providing the range of effort and fire power which would contribute most to the achievement of the common aim. Moreover, he did his best to inculcate this joint approach into his army and corps commanders whom, incidentally, he kept on a very close rein, always deciding himself on the overall strategy and allowing them only to plan, manage and execute particular parts of the current battle, while he turned his attention to the future. He was very lucky in having such sound, professional and loyal subordinates as Miles Dempsey with the 2nd British Army and Omar Bradley with the 1st US, who did everything required of them.

It is sad that Monty's own reputation as our best battlefield General, with the clearest of brains and an invariable master plan, should have lost some credibility by pretending after the event that his strong left flank, held by the British and Canadians, to attract and hold the bulk of the best German Divisions while the Americans captured Cherbourg and exploited to the neck of the Brittany peninsula (which was the basis of that plan), had not essentially included the flat, high ground and the airfields south east of Caen. He always persisted with the story that every one of his limited offensives around Caen which failed to achieve this full degree of expansion had, in fact, gone exactly according to plan and achieved everything he had wanted. To some degree they had, but of course without the airfields which the Allied TAF so badly needed.

One of Monty's problems was that he had to keep up the confidence of both his own troops and the public watching from just across the Channel, and he was extremely short of infantry, who were suffering very heavy casualties in his various offensives and who could not easily be replaced. So he more or less had to make a virtue out of necessity. However, I believe that history should recognise that he was the key figure in the planning and execution of OVERLORD and the architect of victory, and that the attempts emanating at SHAPE to discredit and even go as far as removing him were never justified, even though these were bred from frustration over his self-confident boastfulness and refusal to admit any setbacks at all.

But if Monty was the key figure, the air battle in all its depth and aspects was, perhaps, the critical strategic and tactical factor in OVERLORD's success. Without the Luftwaffe being kept off their backs throughout, without the complex interdiction programme before D-Day and during the bridgehead battle, and without the power of air bombardment at the appropriate place and time, there was no way the land forces were going to get ashore, hold their bridgeheads against fierce counter-attacks and, indeed, break out to Paris and the Seine, hopefully in the process destroying the German armies facing them.

So you could say that the commander of the Allied Expeditionary Air Forces was also an absolutely key appointment. And the man picked early on to fill it, Sir Trafford Leigh-Mallory, the then Commander-in-Chief of Fighter Command (later ADGB), was by no means a bad appointment. Leigh-Mallory was a quiet, frank, generous-hearted and dedicated airman who had been a successful, if somewhat controversial (because of the big wing/small wing argument), commander of 12 Group in the Battle of Britain. He believed passionately in giving the land forces all the support he could muster, in what he recognised would be a difficult and daunting enterprise. But as things worked out he found he had been given one of the most difficult jobs imaginable.

First his responsibilities were ill-defined, in that he was not in full command or even control of all the air effort which could be used in support of OVERLORD. He did control the Two Tactical Air Forces and Air Transport Force, supporting Montgomery and Bradley, but apart from that there was no overall air force chain of command; and he had to go cap in hand to the other air force commands and particularly to the strategic bomber forces if he wanted to obtain further support for ground operations.

Then there were the various characters involved. Leigh-Mallory, with all his qualities, was not a scintillating personality, being rather stolid and, on occasion, inarticulate. For various reasons he was sometimes resented by some of the other commanders in his own service. Friction in the Battle of Britain might have had something to do with it, but it was more that, with the SHAEF hierarchy looking exclusively at OVERLORD, other air commanders might think their own commands were being threatened, and indeed that the more classical use of air power was being put in jeopardy.

First there were the "Bomber Barons" – Harris and Doolittle, even more, Spaatz, who was commander of all the US strategic bomber forces – who took their orders, if they took any at all, from the Combined Chiefs of Staff for whom the British Chief of Air Staff, Portal, acted as coordinator. They all thought, to put no finer point on it, that OVERLORD was the greatest strategic mistake since Germany, according to them, was already tottering on the edge of collapse from night and day bombing and if everyone would only leave them alone and not dissipate their effort they would win the war on their own!

I believe for many reasons they were wrong over this, but it caused them to resent Leigh-Mallory, partly on the grounds that he didn't appreciate the significance of the air war against Germany but, even more, because Harris and Spaatz feared that the strategic forces were going to be hi-jacked by Eisenhower and taken off what they did best. Some compromise was clearly needed because although the strategic bomber offensive was still a long way from bringing Germany to its knees, it was already playing a most significant part in virtually eliminating the Luftwaffe from the skies over Normandy and the Channel by attacking German aircraft production and oil reserves.

Compromise was eventually reached, particularly through incorporating the strategic bomber force into the interdiction programme prior to D-Day and getting them to attack the north-west European, and particularly the French, railway and road network. But Leigh-Mallory was not really the man to achieve this; certainly after D-Day, to get the bombers, who by now were even more reluctant to be taken off their primary role, to carry out direct support of various army assaults it required the intervention of Tedder, who had, in fact, been given the authority by Eisenhower to coordinate the whole strategic and tactical air effort – though he was not always in favour of using bombers to destroy French targets. All this reduced Leigh-Mallory's authority still further.

Nor were his personal relations much better with Tedder above him or with the Tactical Air Force commanders below him. Tedder, who was rather sharper than Leigh-Mallory, and the New Zealander, "Mary" (from the New Zealand "Maori") Coningham, who was a very strong personality indeed, had been together in the Desert and Mediterranean; they were very experienced in every aspect of tactical air support and knew, so to speak, all the cries, which Leigh-Mallory did not. So there was an element of resentment there that he was somehow not 'one of them' – as maybe Margaret Thatcher would have said.

Then there were relations with the Army Group commanders, which added to his troubles. Although, as I said, he was passionately determined to give the land forces all the support he could, he was not invariably appreciated by Montgomery as much as he deserved. This was partly because he had refused, almost certainly quite correctly, to countenance a second airborne assault a month after the first, this time to the south of the Caen battlefield. As a result for a time Monty thought him rather wet, but he forgave him and certainly was prepared to do business with him. The problem was that while Monty very soon set up his own tactical headquarters in Normandy, Leigh-Mallory stayed at Stanmore, which, of course, broke the important Commander-in-Chief's links. So Monty had to make do with a high-powered liaison officer. But this at least produced results, as did the Combined Control Unit at Uxbridge, Coningham's HQ. For it was Coningham, whom Leigh-Mallory had designated Forward Coordinator of both Tactical Air Forces in the early stages of the bridgehead battle, who should have been the man to get right alongside and mark Monty. The trouble was that while Tedder disliked Montgomery, which was to become increasingly obvious with SHAEF's frustrations and machinations about the latter's slowness around Caen, Coningham positively loathed him and the feeling was mutual. This was sad, because up to and including Alamein the two commanders – Commander, Eighth Army and Commander, Desert Air Force – had worked side by side with great success and together had defeated Rommel. But they had fallen out, partly because Monty had resented Coningham giving him gratuitous advice on how he should conduct the pursuit and other operations (a habit he kept up in Normandy), and Coningham had resented Monty for hogging all the limelight after the victory in the Desert! Coningham also became particularly critical of Montgomery's failure to deliver the airfields.

The result was that Monty wouldn't personally work with Coningham, who anyhow, as I say, was at Uxbridge (using the well tried 11 Group communications), and preferred instead to deal either with Leigh-Mallory or, more usually, with the commander of 83 Group, Air Vice-Marshal Harry Broadhurst, who had taken over from Coningham in the Desert and who worked extremely well with the Army. But Broadhurst really should have been supporting – and indeed was supporting – the 2nd Army. Indeed when Dempsey's 2nd Army headquarters moved across to Normandy, Broadhurst immediately set up his own beside him, taking command of all the RAF units over there. So poor Leigh-Mallory must have felt a bit friendless and even at times helpless in his difficult task, yet he did what he could.

Yet despite these personality clashes, the Army/Air control machinery, the planning at Stanmore and the Combined Control Centre at Uxbridge, with 82 ASSU tentacles to all Allied Brigades and airfields at home and in Normandy and G(Air) staff down to Corps, did not work at all badly and the Army continued to rely on, and get, support from the allied air forces in a most remarkable way. These included Bomber Command, brought in after initial resistance from Harris; his cooperation was brilliant and greatly slowed down the Germans' counter-reaction. During and after the landing, although the pre-planned programme was more uncertain and late being agreed, the Allied Air Forces continued to provide (weather permitting – and the weather was foul throughout that June) round the clock support with fighter ground attack and light and medium bombers, all splendidly led at wing and squadron level. This blunted many of the dangerous counter-attacks, particularly on the hard-pressed British sector, and all the time the Luftwaffe, because of the success of the overall air battle, hardly showed up at all.

But as the bridgehead became established and the breaking out became more urgent and difficult, the army looked more and more to the strategic bomber forces to help them punch a hole, and the bombers, with some justification and by now with more and more support from Tedder, became less enthusiastic about diverting their effort from the German cities and industries. They had a point, because when they were used in close support of the land forces they were not always entirely successful, either because they weren't properly followed up with artillery and armoured forces or, on at least two occasions, at St Lo and Falaise, the bombs landed in the wrong place (a case of blue-on-blue). In one case, Caen, which I watched myself at quite close range, they produced so much rubble in the city that actually it made it easier for the defenders and more difficult for us attackers. But they were used; the bombing did numb the German defences for a period and certainly gave them a hard time and contributed to the heavy casualties and strain the Germans were suffering all along the front.

To summarise: the command system, although fraught with difficult personal relations, did eventually work; the air forces knew what they had to do, and the staffs at the higher levels and the leadership at the lower levels got on with the job of destroying German war material. Moreover, continuous and accurate updating of the bomb line proved most important, for it gave the air forces the freedom to attack whatever moved behind them, with whatever was available within the overall mission.

Gentlemen, without the air forces the staggering victory in Normandy, culminating in the Falaise pocket, could not have happened as it did, and, as one of those on the ground who benefited, I salute them.

Chairman

If I may say so, Lord Bramall, the same punchy style that I recall from your time as CDS in the Chiefs of Staff meetings. Thank you very much indeed for that very clear exposition, not only of the command arrangements for OVERLORD – inevitably complex but clearly explained and essential to any understanding of what was going on – and also for your personal touches as someone involved at the time.

Our next speaker is Air Marshal Sir Denis Crowley-Milling, who is going to tell us about the air preparations for OVERLORD – in other words the build-up of the air order of battle, the achievement of air superiority, the air operations that preceded the actual landings, and the support that had to be developed, including for example the construction of airfields in France. He is uniquely qualified to deal with this subject since he not only flew in the Battle of France and in the Battle of Britain but he was in action over Northern France in early 1944, and he formed the first of those vital Typhoon ground attack squadrons that played so vital a part in the whole campaign. Then during the invasion itself he was on the Combined Planning Staff of the 8th USAAF.

Air Vice-Marshal Mike Donaldson, Commandant, greets Field Marshal the Lord Bramall

Left ro right: Sqn Ldr Maria Djumic, Air Chief Marshal Sir Michael Armitage, Major Andy Brown REME, Sqn Ldr Baz Armstrong

"Coffee in the flag room"

Left to right: Sqn Ldr Bob Jenkins, Sqn Ldr Mark Wordley, Wg Cdr Mary Washington-Smith, Sqn Ldr Colin Blagrove, Group Captain Joe Ainsworth RAFHS Gen Secy, Sqn Ldr A Galloway

Wg Cdr Martin Dole, AVM Barry Newton

Coffee time group

Left to right: Group Captain Geoff Thorburn, Wg Cdr Anne Deebank, Wg Cdr Christine Woodman, Dr Christine Goulter, Cecil James

5. *Air Preparations*

Air Marshal Sir Denis Crowley-Milling KCB CBE DSO DFC

John Terraine has set the scene and the Field Marshal has given you a brief insight into the whole operation, the Command arrangements, and how well they did or did not work in practice, a rundown on the leading personalities concerned, and something of the problems and clashes that resulted. He has also generously acknowledged the vital role played by the Allied air forces. It was indeed an overwhelming force, the greatest concentration of air power that has ever been deployed before or since; but whatever went on at the top, at the sharp end it worked and worked well, as it should have done.

The build-up and the air task naturally started long before D-Day with the vital aim of establishing complete air superiority and the minimum opposition to the landings and break out. Air superiority as we know is a continuous battle. Tedder put it very well in his lectures in 1947 on 'Air Power in War': "The fight for air superiority is not a straightforward issue like a naval or land battle; it is not even a series of combats between fighters; it is frequently a highly complex operation which may involve any or all types of aircraft. It is a campaign rather than a battle and there is no absolute finality to it so long as any enemy aircraft are operating." Anyone who was on one of our airfields on the continent at dawn on New Year's Day 1945 will definitely subscribe to that. It was the German air force's final fling with all the elements of surprise and dash, and it created more than a certain amount of havoc. Around 1000 German fighters took part but they lost over 300 in the process. But continuing on this theme, after the war when Field Marshal Von Rundstedt was asked what was the most crucial battle of the war, he replied "the Battle of Britain". The Germans of course failed to gain the essential air superiority before any invasion could be contemplated and this failure made possible the Allies' subsequent re-entry into Europe. It also allowed the bomber force to carry the battle to the heart of Germany and play its part, to be joined later by the 8th Air Force in the campaign for air superiority. For the 8th Air Force, operating in daylight, it was a close run thing, at times suffering quite unacceptable losses.

I was for a short period with the 8th AF Headquarters at Wycombe Abbey (previously the girls' school) and a member of their Combined Operations Planning Committee coordinating fighter escort, but initially of course only at short range. I remember a conference in the Operations Rooms with Generals Doolittle and Anderson; they had just lost 70 aircraft out of force of around 300 attacking Frankfurt. Clearly such a rate could not be sustained and there was an air of gloom. However, the famous P-51B Mustang with the Packard-built Rolls-Royce Merlin engine was beginning to arrive in numbers in 1943, and being superior to the Me109 and Fw190 and with a radius of action of over 600 miles it saved the day. By the spring of 1944 the tide had turned in the daylight air battle over Germany, allowing round the clock bombing by the combined strategic bomber force and tying up Ack-Ack, fighters, radar and thousands of personnel that might have been thrown against the invasion, let alone destroying German aircraft production and airfields. As a result, on D-Day the estimated 600 sorties that our intelligence judged could be flown against the landings turned out to be far less – around 200 – and quite ineffectual.

The "Trident" conference in Washington in May 1943 set 1 May 1944 for the invasion, but which time the Combined Chiefs of Staff had issued a new directive, Point Blank, and this tied the strategic force for the first time to OVERLORD. And you know what Harris and Spaatz's reaction was to that.

Leigh-Mallory was solely responsible for planning the air side of OVERLORD and it became clear that in order to isolate the invasion area the strategic bombers would be required. The Transportation Plan, mainly devised by Zuckerman (brought in by Tedder), aimed to create a railway desert within 150 miles of Caen, about which you will hear more later. Leigh-Mallory, though nominally responsible for the success or failure of the air plan, was given no power in his directive to control the strategic force, and they did not exactly welcome the idea of being directed by him. In fact, though appointed in April 1943, he received no directive until November and was told the question of the control of strategic forces had yet to be resolved. Eventually Eisenhower did so, bringing in Tedder as his deputy, and the strategic forces finally came under direct control of SHAPE, but not until 14 April 1944.

I will turn now to the build-up of 2 TAF, a force based on the experience in North Africa with the 8th Army and the Desert Air Force. There is no doubt Montgomery was quick to appreciate air power and never moved a foot without it. I was present at a briefing given by him at Camberley on his return from North Africa. He curtly informed us that he had rewritten the principles of war, and that his first principle of war was, as he put it, to win his air battle. He then went on to expound on the need for the two Commanders to be alongside each other (which of course did not work out on OVERLORD with Coningham) and for there to be a joint Army/Air plan. 21 Army Group's Directive on the use of air power reflected this. It had worked well in the desert using both fighters and light bombers in close support of the ground forces, all working to the joint plan. A similar set-up was required for OVERLORD, but with improvements on the signals side.

In fact Leigh-Mallory was involved in planning as early as 1942 (SLEDGEHAMMER) when AOC 11 Group and later as C-in-C Fighter Command, and he proposed that 2 TAF be formed within his Command. At that time on the signals side his right-hand man was Wing Commander Porter, now Air Marshal Sir Kenneth Porter who is with us today, and I am grateful to him for an input to my talk. Altogether Ken Porter spent a crucial 18 months with Leigh-Mallory and holds a different view of him in certain respects to that expounded by some historians. As early as January 1943 (before his appointment) Leigh-Mallory took a team to North Africa consisting of Dickson (AOC 83 Gp, designate), Groom (SASO 2 TAF, designate) and Ken Porter to study the Army/Air set-up and control.

By this time the new ground attack fighter squadrons had already started forming in Fighter Command. In fact I formed the first Typhoon bomber squadron (181) in September 1942. Rocket projectiles came much later. The Typhoon was not exactly a happy aircraft to start with; initially the tail had a habit of coming off, it had a rather vicious high speed stall in a combat turn, and you never knew when the engine was going to pack up. The squadron suffered 26 forced landings due to engine failure in the first month or so. Anyway they eventually got it right, but failed to appreciate that an engine intake filter would be required to stop the fine dust of the Normandy soil damaging the sleeve valve engine. It became a superb close support aircraft, built like a battleship, and could take a great deal of punishment.

It was Leigh-Mallory who first proposed building airfields along the south coast of England like New Romney and Dungeness and by mid 1943 we were operating off the same type of airfields the Royal Engineers Airfield Construction Companies would be building in Normandy, hopefully soon after D-Day. By this time we were all living under canvas. Our main occupation at this stage was dive-bombing and strafing airfields in Northern France, some around Caen. We were initially controlled by 11 Group Operations but later taken over by 83 Group as the new Group built up at Gatwick Park from March 1943 with its Group Control Centre. So we come to the Mobile Operations Room Units and Mobile Air Reporting Units. Ken Porter, who wrote the signal plan for ROUNDUP and OVERLORD – and TORCH also – started forming MORUs and MARUs in late 1942 and subjected them to intensive mobility training day and night. As a result of the visit to the Desert Air Force, Porter felt he could improve on the signals side of the organisation and it was he who brought in the RAF forward controller equipped with VHF to call down patrolling aircraft on to army targets – a 'cab rank' as it became known – and it proved highly successful. There were some controllers in the leading tanks.

In March 1943 we took part in the first major invasion exercise, Exercise SPARTAN, planned by GOC-in-C South Eastern Command, involving the first Canadian Army and its two Corps in the Southampton area. It assumed a break out following the assault. This was an ideal opportunity to try out the new signals set-up in a mobile situation. In fact it all functioned rather too well, and both units were promptly moved abroad to support the Sicily landings supposedly on loan, but never to be returned. At this stage I must also mention the RAF Servicing Commando Units, which were also building up and some took part in the exercise. They would be the first to service aircraft on the landing strips in Normandy.

In June 1943 2 TAF Headquarters was formed here at Bracknell under Air Marshal D'Albiac. Coningham was still involved in the Mediterranean, and did not take over until February 1944, when the Headquarters moved to Uxbridge. Meanwhile, Broadhurst had taken over from Dickson at 83 Group. Coningham was to command both 2 TAF and 9th US Air Force during the assault and set up an Advanced Headquarters AEAF. He certainly looked upon AEAF as a tiresome extra Headquarters in the chain of command.

Turning to the detailed organisation, 83 and 84 Groups were built up identically with 29 squadrons, followed by 85 (air defence) Group, including night-fighter Mosquitos. Fighter Command then reverted to its old title of ADGB, and very busy it was with high level standing patrols far out in the Channel for many weeks in all weather before D-Day to stop German recce aircraft flying over southern England as the invasion forces built up. 2 TAF also included 2 Group, which was detached from Bomber Command on 1 June 1943. I shall of course be referring to other air force units as General Crookenden and I later discuss the detailed plan, the assault and the break out. For example 100 Group which was formed in Bomber Command in November 1943 had a major part in the deception plan. Nor must we forget Coastal Command, or the Transport Force of 38 and 46 Groups, or the special duties squadrons at Tempsford, part of 3 Group, Bomber Command.

I finally leave you with some statistics to think about. By June 1944 the RAF, including Commonwealth elements, had over 8,300 aircraft, 487 squadrons and 1,170,000 personnel. The Allied Air Forces totalled 11,400 aircraft of which over 600 were transports.

Chairman

Our speakers are building a very firm foundation for our study of the campaign, and Denis has now brought us much closer to the air side of OVERLORD. It's been particularly valuable to hear from someone who was not only fighting in the front line but also served on the air staff at this very important time.

We are now going to have two presentations given by Air Marshal Sir Denis Crowley-Milling and by Lieutenant General Sir Napier Crookenden, another soldier who was in the thick of the fighting on D-Day. He was Brigade Major of the 6th Air Landing Brigade, a formation that went in early on D-Day in gliders to hold the southern end of the 6th Airborne Division bridgehead against 21st Panzer Division. A month later he took command of a Parachute Battalion and he subsequently took part in the air drops at the Rhine Crossings, where he won the DSO. Like Lord Bramall General Crookenden is a military historian of note, and many of us will have read his history of the British Airborne Divisions in OVERLORD – which encompasses his own 6th Airborne Division and also the 82nd and 101st American. The joint presentation they are now going to give – a box and cox across the stage – will be on planning the operation.

6. Planning the Operation

Lieutenant General Sir Napier Crookenden KCB DSO OBE DL and Air Marshal Sir Denis Crowley-Milling KCB CBE DSO DFC

NC: We have heard from John Terraine of the remarkable fact that the offensive planning for a return to the continent began as early as 1940 and of the mass of preliminary work on plans, material and techniques accomplished by Lord Mountbatten and his Combined Operations Staff. In January 1943 the planning process took a giant step forward, when the Prime Minister, the President and their Chiefs of Staff met at Casablanca and ordered that detailed planning for OVERLORD should now begin.

Through that summer of 1943 frequent arguments and continuous discussions went on. Unexpected support for an invasion in the Pas de Calais popped up from some of the army planners, only to be violently opposed by the Americans. A senior officer in the army's Home Forces questioned the need for OVERLORD at all –

D C-M: well briefed by Spaatz and Harris no doubt!

NC: but in the end agreement was reached and on 15 July 1943 COSSAC delivered to the British Chiefs of Staff an "OUTLINE OVERLORD PLAN."

D C-M: In essence the air plan covered four over-lapping stages. First, the strategic bombing of Germany, POINTBLANK, was to continue, but the directive was modified to take in OVERLORD. The second stage consisted of targets more closely connected with the invasion. The third concerned the assault phase – the air giving protection to the sea and land forces across the Channel, and when ashore. The fourth phase was the prevention and delaying of the arrival of reinforcements, and the direct support of the land forces in the bridgehead.

The main essential was a favourable air situation. Total enemy air in the area was estimated at just under 2,000 aircraft with a maximum effort of less than 900, which on the day proved to be by a long way over optimistic. Before the assault, the bombing of railway centres, coastal batteries, and airfields within at least 130 miles of the beaches would be necessary. Leigh-Mallory's planners at an early stage realised that this would be beyond the capability of the tactical air forces. Another essential was the provision of airfields in the Caen area early after the landings and in the area west of Paris to enable us to operate over the Seine in strength to meet the anticipated German counter-attack – a matter reinforced by Montgomery at all his briefings. Caen, however, was not captured until 10 July.

NC: Limited as the planners were by the resources allotted to them, the plan called for a seaborne assault by three divisions with an immediate follow-up by two more divisions and with two-thirds of an airborne division on the flanks. The COSSAC staff had themselves realised that this proposed assault force was only marginally adequate and they called for an all-round increase in landing ships and craft and in transport aircraft.

Later in August the QUADRANT conference in Quebec approved the OVERLORD plan and ordered the COSSAC staff to get on with detailed planning.

D C-M: On 6 December President Roosevelt announced that General Eisenhower would be the Supreme Allied Commander for OVERLORD and on 31 December at Marakesh General Montgomery was given a copy of the OVERLORD outline plan by Mr Churchill. He had already been asked by Eisenhower to return to the UK as soon as possible, together with Eisenhower's Chief of Staff, Major General Bedell Smith, there to revise the OVERLORD plan with Leigh-Mallory and Admiral Ramsay, the appointed Naval Commander.

NC: Montgomery and Eisenhower at once insisted that the assault planned by COSSAC was on too narrow a front; that five assault divisions were essential; that the landing beaches should be extended to the eastern shore of the Cherbourg Peninsula; and that three airborne divisions were required, two on the western flank and one on the eastern. At a conference on 21 January in St Paul's School on its old site in Hammersmith, each C-in-C explained the new air, naval and army plans and the additional air, naval and army resources now required. In this statement of the army's requirements for air action Montgomery included the reduction of the Luftwaffe, the concealment of the Allied intentions by air attack on targets outside the OVERLORD target area, bombing of the rail network to prevent enemy movement from the east, and air attack on the landing areas from D minus 1.

D C-M: At this stage Leigh-Mallory responded with a detailed target plan, which primarily was the work of Professor Zuckerman, whom Tedder had brought back from the Mediterranean where he had produced a similar plan for Sicily and Italy. The team also included an expert on the French railways, Mr Brand, and Mr Lawrence of the Ministry of Economic Warfare. The plan included seventeen rail centres chosen for attack. Altogether seventy-five targets were listed, including bridges, to isolate the battle area, and clearly it required a tonnage on many targets that only the strategic force could deliver.

Harris, as we have heard, got wind of this, and produced a paper for CAS and others casting doubt on Bomber Command's ability to take on targets requiring such accuracy. Also he considered it an unnecessary diversion from the main task of his force. However, he was persuaded to carry out a trial bombing of six French railway marshalling yards, which took place on the night 6/7 March 1944 and was in every way a striking success.

The Command dropped 1,258 tons and it was over a month before the yards were operating again. These results helped greatly in the arguments in favour of the plan, though fear of French civilian casualties, somewhat overestimated at 80 to 160,000, had the Prime Minister and the War Cabinet wavering, and they called for a reduction in the number of centres to be attacked. Eisenhower insisted that the isolation of the battlefield was vital to success; moreover the casualty figure was considerably downgraded as information filtered back from France following the trial bombing attacks. The plan was finally adopted in April and Tedder informed Harris and Spaatz, issuing them with details of the targets to be attacked by their forces.

NC: I might add that only a week before D-Day there was intense concern at 21 Army Group about the implementation of the air plan, in which considerable doubt still existed about the role of the heavy bombers and the completion of the transportation plan. At 3 pm on 3 June Montgomery telephoned Leigh-Mallory to ask if there was any change in the air plan and Leigh-Mallory replied that he would resign rather than agree to any. That same day Brigadier Richardson, Montgomery's Brigadier Ops, was sent by Montgomery to the final conference at Headquarters AEAF, where Tedder voiced some criticisms of the communications bombing plan and supported Harris and Spaatz in advocating more attacks on German airfields. However, Leigh-Mallory stuck to his guns and the communications attacks went on. General Charles Richardson would have been with us today but for his recent death, and his lively mind and vivid memories of the Desert War and of D-Day would have been invaluable.

In 1942, on his arrival in North Africa, Montgomery had immediately moved his headquarters to beside Coningham's Desert Air Force and there followed a model of army/air control of operations. The two commanders worked closely together and Charles Richardson, then the Army's GS01 in the Joint Ops Room, told me how close, effective and cheerful relations were at all levels – a situation made even better with the arrival as AOC of Harry Broadhurst.

In 1944 Montgomery and Leigh-Mallory got on well together, if you except an occasional spat, but Coningham found it difficult to cope with Montgomery's habit of running a battle from a small, advanced tactical headquarters. Both Tedder and Coningham disliked Montgomery's assertive manner, although both are on record as saying that Monty towered above any other soldier in his appreciation of the air weapon. However, it is worth making clear that army/air cooperation at the working level was generally good. Under the sensible leadership of Broadhurst in 83 Group and Dempsey in Second Army, army/air relations were excellent and most effective – and the same can be said of 84 Group and First Canadian Army.

D C-M: For the attacks against coastal batteries a joint naval/air plan was devised. On the air side in the attacks leading up to D-Day, two batteries were to be attacked in the Pas de Calais and Dieppe areas for every one in Normandy – to keep the Germans guessing. By 5 June 16,000 tons covering twenty-one batteries in the NEPTUNE area alone had been delivered. At the same time there would be spoof raids, dropping dummy parachute troops and fire crackers.

NC: From the beginning of COSSAC planning the problem of deceiving the Germans on the assault area had been studied and eventually Operation FORTITUDE was implemented. Throughout the first three months of 1944 a phantom US Fourth Army group was built up in Kent and East Anglia with General Patton in command and MI5 and the British XX Committee directed the operations of twenty captured and "turned" enemy agents to convince the Germans that we were going to land in the Pas de Calais. FORTITUDE was successful and the Germans from Hitler down to Rommel and his two army commanders remained convinced until mid-July that the main invasion was still to come in the Pas de Calais, where the German 15th Army still awaited us.

D C-M: I have already referred to the formation of 100 Group in November 1943, with the task of confounding and destroying enemy electronic defences. The plan was to produce what was called a MANDREL screen to cover the actual invasion and a further, similar screen covering a dummy invasion off the Pas de Calais. 617 Squadron, led by Leonard Cheshire, was one of the squadrons involved and it required extremely accurate but rather tedious flying to provide the right illusion of a further assault force approaching. The Group also had the task of destroying airborne electronic defences.

Attacks planned against German electronic centres in late May and early June proved very successful. Sixty transmitters in the Boulogne area were almost wiped out by 105 Lancasters. HQ German Signals Intelligence Centre was completely wiped out and twenty-one long-range reporting stations were also destroyed. Typhoons of 83 and 84 Groups were also involved in forty-two attacks on radar stations in the week before D-Day. So there was no early warning and no enemy aircraft hindered the airborne operations.

All this time, of course, thousands upon thousands of photographs – beaches and exits, airfields, dropping and landing sites, as well as parks, dumps, and radar installations – were being taken by 2 TAF Recce Wings, some at extremely low level and hazardous. Always as many or more sorties were carried out in the Pas de Calais area as in Normandy for the two weeks before D-Day. One RAF Field Mobile Photo Section alone developed more than 120,000 prints for use by the army.

NC: One vertical photograph I shall never forget came into the 6 Airborne Division/38 Group Joint Planning HQ on 17 April. It showed a mass of white dots all over our planned dropping and landing zones; these were holes for the erection of anti-air landing poles. For a moment we thought that the gaff was blown, but subsequent photos showed similar holes all along the French coast. General Gale relegated us to the second lift in the evening.

The army plan called for the landing of three airborne divisions on D-Day, the American 82nd and 101st on the Cherbourg Peninsula and the British 6th east of the Orne river. Joint planning for the operations of the latter began in February in a secure house at Milston within a mile of both 38 Group and 6th Airborne Division Headquarters. Shortage of aircraft made landing in two lifts unavoidable and even then 46 Group reached the necessary strengths only after strenuous efforts by Air Marshal Leslie Hollinghurst.

The first lift consisted of the two parachute brigades, whose main bodies were to drop at 0050, followed at 0300 by a first landing of sixty-eight Horsa and 4 Hamilcar gliders. The second lift with the 6th Air Landing Brigade in 258 Horsas and Hamilcars was to land at 2100.

Planning went less smoothly for the American airborne divisions. Leigh-Mallory disliked the whole plan and prophesied that "casualties will not only prove fatal to the success of the operations itself, but will also jeopardise all future airborne operations . . . you are throwing away two airborne divisions". General Bradley insisted that these two divisions were essential to the seaborne landings on UTAH beach. He was supported by Montgomery and Eisenhower and when the success of these two divisions was known on D-Day, Leigh-Mallory wrote at once to say how delighted he was to be proved wrong.

D C-M: Let us now look at some of the Air Force tasks. Coastal Command had fifty-one squadrons plus twelve further squadrons, a mixture of Fleet Air Arm, US Navy and RCAF. It covered surface vessels and U-Boat movements from Norway to Brest. In fact during the four days before D-Day a total of 6,875 mines were laid together by Coastal and Bomber Commands, causing a heavy risk to all German shipping movements.

However, while all the planning and preliminary operations were taking place, a new menace reared its head in early 1943. Reports were received of trials of a secret weapon – the flying bomb (and later the V2 rocket) – and attacks by Bomber Command on the centre identified at Peenemunde were started in August 1943, which we learned later set back production some weeks. In October reports reached Intelligence that "a concrete platform with a centre axis pointing directly at London was being constructed near Abbeville".

We now know that they planned to build 5,000 V1s a month and to saturate London with them. Under Operation CROSSBOW aircraft from all air forces were diverted to attack V1 sites, code-named NOBALL. By May 1944 103 out of 140 sites had been destroyed. The first V1 flying bomb was not launched on London until 12 June 1944, but it then built up into a continuous assault. In one month from 15 June to 15 July 1,280 fell inside the London area and this went on until early September, when the Allied armies overran most of the sites. It was indeed a serious diversion of effort involving at its height fifteen day-fighter and six night-fighter squadrons entirely on DIVER patrols, over 2,000 balloons, 592 heavy and 922 light AA guns. This formidable effort finally reduced the success rate following launch to as low as 17%. The Germans switched to air launching and then came the V2 rocket, but that is another story.

We must come back to decision time for D-Day.

D C-M: In the evening of 5 June two Typhoon pilots of 245 Squadron, 212 Wing, 83 Group, based at Holmsey South, were briefed to carry out a weather recce. They were to fly south of Brest to report on cloud conditions in the area. They were under strict R/T silence and under no circumstances were they to engage enemy aircraft or to shoot up anything at sea. They did notice a couple of high-ranking army officers at the briefing, but nothing was said. It seemed to them just another routine weather check. Little did they know that the decision to go had already been taken at 0415 that morning. Even at the top there had been so many dummy practices in taking such a decision and then seeing how conditions actually worked out that some people in the chain did not at first believe it was for real.

NC: In fact at 2145 on 4 June General Eisenhower overrode Montgomery's insistence on sticking to the original D-Day of 5 June and ordered a 24-hour postponement. With equal firmness, at 0415 next morning, he brushed aside Leigh-Mallory and ignored Tedder's uncertainty in giving the word GO for 6 June. Most of the ships were already at sea and by midnight on 5 June the British and American airborne troops were less than an hour away from their drop zones.

Thirty minutes into D-Day the first thousand bombs from Bomber Command Lancasters fell on the Merville Battery. The invasion had begun.

Chairman

Admirable jointery, and a very clear presentation of how the invasion plan was developed. Once again for one of our Historical Society study days Dr Horst Boog has come across from Freiburg where he was until very recently the Chief Historian of the Military History Research Office. Dr Boog's first experience of the RAF was when he found himself under its bombs during the war, towards the end of which he trained as a glider pilot and joined the Volkssturm. He then followed a career as an interpreter, was at Nuremberg, served in intelligence, and became an historian. He has written many important reference books, some of which are now being published in English in this country. They are outstanding material. We look forward to hearing from you about the Luftwaffe situation in 1944 and its response to the Normandy invasion.

7. *The Luftwaffe Role – Situation and Response*

Dr Horst Boog

(Editor's Note: In the limited time available Dr Boog could only summarise the paper he had written for the seminar. In view of its interest to Society members and to military historians in general we reproduce it in full here, together with the references.)

Introduction

Hitler's political and military strategy in the spring of 1944 rested on his hope – or delusion – that the new weapons under development, like the buzz bomb, the V2 rocket, the He 177 long-range bomber, the Me 262 and Ar 234 jet aircraft, and the new types of U-boat, could change the course of the war to Germany's advantage. Since invasion was imminent in the west, where space could not be traded for time on account of the insufficient operational depth, all available forces must be concentrated there to counter it, while the fronts in the east and in Italy had to be held at all costs and as far away from Germany as possible in order to prevent any increase of the air threat. An invasion must be repelled by every possible method in its first crucial hours. Once the Allies were defeated there, it was assumed they would not venture a similar undertaking again in the foreseeable future. Hitler could then reconquer the lost territory in the east and finally establish his continental empire on an "ethnically cleansed" (as we would say today) racial basis to avoid for ever an internal collapse of Germany like the one of 1918. Germany would then be prepared to fight for world hegemony.

The Luftwaffe and Overlord

When the Wehrmacht launched its onslaught against the Soviet Union in June 1941, the air defence of western Europe was left to only two fighter Geschwader. It was expected that the campaign in the east would be short and that strong fighter forces could be shifted westwards after three to four months. But the campaign in the east became a war of attrition. The Chief of the Luftwaffe General Staff therefore said in the spring of 1942, when all hopes for a speedy victory in the east were gone, that first the war in Russia had to be won before more attention could be given again to the training of flying crews.[1] Goring later complained: "What went to the east never came back. It remained there."[2] In May 1944, however, the development of new jets and rockets and the increasing fighter production put him in a euphoric mood,[3] which was quite unjustified, because the secret weapons were still far from mass production.

What happened in between in the west? In the winter of 1941/2 the question of how to defend Germany's rear in the west began to occupy Hitler's attention. In December 1941 he had ordered the construction of the "Atlantic Wall"[4] and in March 1942[5] he had settled the question of command authority in the western coastal areas and their defence in order to cope with the possibility of Allied landing operations. In accordance with his general policy of "divide et impera!", preventing anyone from gaining too much power and becoming dangerous to the dictator, he did not establish a theatre commander with control over all the services in the west. C-in-C West remained a territorial commander and commander of the army units only. Luftwaffe and navy units remained under their own Cs-in-C but were asked to cooperate with the army. So IIIrd Flak Corps, which was mainly employed against tanks in ground warfare, was subordinated to Air Fleet 3.

The system was later to cause much confusion,[6] which was increased by the so-called "tank controversy"[7] mainly between Field Marshal Rommel, C-in-C of Army Group B in northern France, and General Geyr von Schweppenburg, C-in-C of Panzergruppe West. Not knowing where exactly the main invasion would take place, the former wanted to deploy the tank units along the Channel coast in order to fend off landings in the critical first hours, while the tank general wanted their concentrated employment as soon as the main thrust was clearly recognised. For this the tank units would have to be deployed centrally farther inland. Both views had their advantages and disadvantages, which cannot be discussed here. Hitler's decision of 26 April 1944[8] was a compromise. He gave Rommel, who had depended mostly on infantry units, three tank divisions to be stationed along the coast and thus weakened the tank reserves of C-in-C West under Panzergruppe West, whose tank units were to be released to the battle front by the Supreme Command of the Armed Forces, ie by Hitler, only if considered necessary. Together with the unsubstantiated belief that the main invasion would take place in the Dunkirk–Calais area – a belief that lasted until early August 1944[9] and rested not only on the successful deception by "Fortitude South",[10] but also on faulty reconnaissance and signal intelligence as well as on the fact that this would be the shortest approach to the industrial centre of the Ruhr and would hit the V1 and V2 launching sites directly – this arrangement had to be blamed later on for the piecemeal melting away of the tank divisions. Always too few were released for combat too late.

There were of course other reasons for the gradual decimation, like the overwhelming Allied air supremacy and the guns of the ships reaching 10 km farther than expected. It must be added here that all army plans for the shifting of supplies, and reinforcements of troops were characterised by a conspicuous disregard for the impact of enemy air power. With Directive No. 51 and subsequent orders of November 1943 to January 1944[11] Hitler reminded the armed forces in the west that the outcome of an invasion would be decisive for the war and ordered them to intensify their defensive preparations. Above all he forbade any further use of the forces in the west as bases for supplying other theatres of war with personnel and material. The Luftwaffe was ordered to throw its home defence fighter and mobile flak forces, plus training units and reserves, into the invasion area in case of an Allied landing; and to expand its ground organisation in the west and disperse its airfields in order to protect itself against, and split up, the attacking air forces of the enemy.[12]

The uncertainty about the geographical site of an invasion created by insufficient air reconnaissance and the lack of reliable intelligence caused the Luftwaffe to prepare for every eventuality in western, southern and south-eastern Europe.[13] Contingency planning ranged from Norway via Denmark, the north German coast, the Netherlands, the Channel coast, Brittany, Biscay, the French Mediterranean coast and the Adriatic coast to Greece and Bulgaria, not forgetting Portugal and Spain. All measures pertaining to the defence of the west were known under the code name "Drohende Gefahr West" (Danger Threat West) and were first formulated in a directive of the C-in-C Luftwaffe of 27 July 1943, ie immediately after the Allied invasion of Sicily, to be replaced by another directive of 27 February 1944 and amended many times in accordance with new situations until April 1944.[14] Like Hitler, Goering believed that warding off any landing attempt would be decisive for the later course of the war and that, in view of the initial weakness of an amphibious attacker on the coast, concentrated employment of all flying forces in the first hours of a landing operation would be imperative. Immediate reinforcement of Air Fleet 3 commanding all Luftwaffe forces in the west was therefore necessary. Air Fleet Reich, responsible for home air defence, disliked being stripped of nearly all its fighter forces because its commander, Generaloberst Stumpff, regarded air defence as one entity that should not be split up. Of course he had to comply but managed to retain control over the 3rd Fighter Division stationed in Belgium and the Netherlands, the main route of Allied bomber forces into Germany.[15]

The main tasks of Field Marshal Sperrle's Air Fleet 3 in case of invasion were to establish air superiority over the army combat zone with a sufficient number of interceptors, to attack enemy ships and troops on the beaches with fighters and fighter bombers during daytime – 8 Fighter Gruppen of Air Fleet Reich had to be equipped with bomb-carrying appliances for this purpose, and Hitler had even promised Rommel a thousand Me 262 jet fighters for this job[16] – and to do the same at night with bombers; as experience in Sicily and Italy had shown, these could not be employed without heavy fighter cover by day. Heavy bombers with guided bombs were to be used against floating as well as land targets.

So the overall role of the Luftwaffe in the west was to support the ground forces. It was planned to train the fighter pilots, who were supposed to fly up to five sorties daily in the first days, for the support role and to familiarise them in advance with the terrain and the location of the camouflaged airfields and forward landing grounds reserved for them when they were switched from home air defence to fight the invasion.[17] 3 Air Fleet had about 100 airfields and auxiliary landing grounds available within a radius of 350 miles from Normandy, those near Paris being particularly well suited. There were not enough, however, to cope also with the transfers and to allow for the possibility of the Allies bombing them prior to the invasion.

More airfields were needed for dispersal and to maintain the operability of the flying forces at all costs. But there was a great dilemma. The army insisted on the destruction of airfields close to the coast for fear of airborne operations and Allied air supremacy in that area. The Luftwaffe therefore operated few airfields within 100 km of the coast. Most fighters and fighter bombers were stationed north and northeast of Paris, the bombers farther south. German fighters thus were at a disadvantage and the need for drop tanks to make up for their short ranges excluded their use as fighter bombers.

Another factor was that the ground organisation was short of labour and resources and showed little initiative; they had been spoilt by the good life of France after 1940, which had prevented the necessary expansion, although the staff of the IInd Fliegerkorps, which was transferred from Italy in the winter of 1943/4, gave new impetus based on their experience in combating Allied air superiority.[18] The new airfield projects therefore took better account of the need for camouflage, dispersal of revetments, and interconnecting roads to combine several airfields and runways into large airfields, within which the aircraft could be shunted while the control centres were placed outside them, but the system was far from completion by June 1944. The region south and west of the actual landing zone was, in particular, rather short of airfields. The location of many fighter and fighter-bomber airfields east of the invasion area constituted another operational disadvantage: the fighters had to approach the battlefield mainly from the east which facilitated the surveillance of this flank by the Allies.[19]

Field Marshal Sperrle's Air Fleet 3 consisted of several commands:

a. Fliegerkorps X at Angers had been transferred from Greece in March 1944 and had absorbed the staff of Fliegerfuhrer Atlantik, whose submarine support and anti-shipping operations it continued with only 19 serviceable long-range bombers and a few long-range reconnaissance planes, all of which had insufficient range for warfare over the Atlantic.

b. IXth Fliegerkorps at Le Coudray had the young General Peltz in command; he had earlier been Angriffsfuhrer England (attack leader England). By order of Hitler he had resumed German bombing operations against Britain in 1943 and commanded the Baby Blitz of winter and spring 1944. In January 1944 he had 462 operational aircraft but his forces, mostly two-engine medium bombers, were exhausted by May and comprised only 107 operational aircraft of which 35 were fighter-bombers. His attack forces had never averaged more than 200 planes and had suffered great losses from the British defences. The pre-invasion raids from 27 to 29 May against the ports of Weymouth, Torquay and Falmouth could only be carried out by 50 to 60 planes each time.

c. 2 Flieger Division was in southern France, mainly equipped with torpedo planes for anti-shipping operations in the western Mediterranean. Its operational strength in late May was 72 aircraft.

d. IInd Fighter Corps at Chantilly under General Werner Junck was in command of all fighter and night-fighter units in France. Its only two day-fighter Geschwader, 2 and 26,[20] had been in combat along the Channel coast since 1940 and suffered high losses so there was a severe shortage of experienced pilots. Some weak forces, three Gruppen in all, were deployed north of Paris and near Lille. The few twin-engine fighters in Brittany had to be left without single-engine fighter protection. Some units had to be shifted farther south-east to evade constant attacks by fighters escorting the bomber streams which had forced them to take off too early each time with the consequence that they did not have enough fuel for later air combat.

e. Finally there was the IInd Fliegerkorps in Compiegne under General Buelowius. This had to prepare the ground organisation for later ground support operations. It was just a staff without any fighter-bomber units and therefore could not practise cooperation with the army.[21] Nor could III Flak Corps exercise anti-tank combat.[22]

Ten days before the invasion 3 Air Fleet had an actual strength of 919 aircraft, 510 of which were serviceable. Among them were 240/125 fighters, 360/198 bombers, 40/27 ground attack planes, 86/51 night-fighters, 136/72 reconnaissance aircraft and 57/37 heavy fighters/destroyers.[23]

This force was too feeble to oppose the Allied pre-invasion bombing effectively, once the introduction of the long-range escort fighters had secured Allied air supremacy in the spring of 1944. German day-fighter losses in home air defence against Allied forces eight times their strength in March–May 1944 averaged 10.8% each month. Germany's aircraft losses from all causes in the first five months of 1944 amounted to twice the Luftwaffe's total strength, ie about 13,300, 6,000 of them through enemy action.[24] German fighter pilot losses in this period had risen from 12.1% to 25%, ie they had reached a figure of 2,262 or 99% of the average fighter pilot strength.[25] These figures also reflect the insufficient flying training of the pilots, which had to be reduced on account of the 'fuel famine' as far back as summer 1942 and was now only 40% of its pre-war duration or about one-third of that given to an Allied fighter pilot. For these reasons the quality of the average fighter pilot was bad, and most were not trained in blind flying.[26]

Big Week had reduced German fighter production from 1,531

aircraft in January 1944 to 1,202 in February, and although the output surged to 1,714 in March and 3,110 in September 1944, there were only 587 single-engine and 126 twin-engine fighters available for home air defence in late May 1944, 333 and 53 of which respectively were operational. The other theatres of war also had to be supplied, and many fighter pilots were not fully combat ready.

In short, thanks to these weaknesses, the Allied air forces were not only able to paralyse railroad facilities and destroy many bridges across the Seine, but also bomb about 36 airfields within a distance of 130 miles from Caen, forcing the Luftwaffe to operate its fighters and bombers from bases farther away.[27]

The absolute air supremacy of the Allies long before the invasion took place also prevented the Luftwaffe from continuous photo reconnaissance over the invasion bases. Only 129 sporadic reconnaissance flights over the Channel and southern coast of England were possible in the six weeks before the landing, and although the preparations for invasion did not escape Luftwaffe attention, it came as a tactical surprise.[28] On D-Day about 319 serviceable aircraft of 3 Air Fleet, among them about 100 fighters, were confronted with more than 12,800 Allied aircraft, which made not only Air Chief Marshal Leigh-Mallory but also the German ground troops ask: "Where is the Luftwaffe?".[29]

General Junck, Commanding General of II Fighter Corps, had, in view of the Allied bombing operations against bridges and transportation in northern France, asked for the planned fighter reinforcements as early as the end of April. But the Luftwaffe High Command needed all its fighters to fend off the air offensive against the German synthetic gasoline industry beginning on 12 May. The synthetic oil plants produced more than 90% of the Luftwaffe's aviation fuel, production of which dropped from 178,000 tons in April 1944 to only 53,000 tons in June and 10,000 in September 1944, against a consumption of 195,000 tons in May. Flight restrictions therefore had to be imposed in June, although the lack of aviation fuel came to be really felt at the front only in September thanks to the 580,000 tons in stock. These supplies, however, could no longer easily be transported to where they were needed because of the growing dislocation of the transportation system and shortage of motor vehicles. So the increased fighter production could not have the desired effect on the combat readiness of the fighter forces at the front.[30] Thus the threat against German aviation fuel and the general shortage of forces caused the Luftwaffe High Command to postpone the planned transfer of about 16 to 19 Gruppen (approximately 800 fighters) mainly from the home air defence command to France until the last possible moment. Eight of these Gruppen were to be put under II Fliegerkorps as fighter bombers. One reason why the Luftwaffe considered this transfer feasible in the event of invasion was the belief that the Allies would then throw all their flying forces, including the strategic bombers, into the decisive ground battle – a policy that would have been mandatory under German air doctrine.[31] This was a good example of the dangers of projecting one's own ideas on the opponent; unfortunately the opponent had so many aircraft that the expected short relief over Germany did not take place.

On 6 June 1944 the Luftwaffe in the west had to fight against an Allied air force about forty times its strength. German planes hardly succeeded in penetrating the Allied air umbrella over the landing zone.[32] Only twelve fighter-bombers reached this area, and ten of them had to release their bombs prematurely. The only success worth mentioning was a hit on a ship directing Allied aircraft. The transfer of reinforcements from Germany was ordered – and for reasons of weather and Allied air supremacy took place very late, because initially there was much uncertainty about the main invasion thrust. This transfer, when it started on 7 June, developed into a drama lasting almost three days. Fatally, Air Fleet Reich had been unable previously to spare pilots of the units earmarked for transfer so that they could be familiarised with their routes and the locations of their assigned airfields – many of which had been bombed in the meantime. In addition the day-fighter pilots, having been stationed on well maintained airfields at home with all necessary facilities, had difficulties in finding their way to improvised forward landing grounds and in navigating on their own. They were accustomed to being guided by radio and radar during home defence missions. In France, however, the radio connections had been largely destroyed. Moreover radio silence had to be maintained during transfer. In the event the higher staffs lost control of their flying units. Leaving behind for home defence just four Gruppen and some smaller industrial alert or training units – altogether about 180 single-engine and 150 twin-engine fighters with rather inexperienced crews – the fighter units no longer constituted the force they had been at home. Flying low to avoid enemy fighters and radar, they frequently lost orientation during transfer flights and failed to find their airfields. Many pilots baled out for lack of fuel, others crash-landed on bombed runways, many were shot down by friend or foe.[33] Of fifty-seven fighter planes despatched from Wiesbaden to Evreux only three arrived, forty-seven landed or crash-landed elsewhere, and seven went missing. Of twenty-two Fw

190 fighters flying from Cologne to Villacoublay only two arrived.[34] The transfer was a disaster.

Its reinforcement by 800 fighters and fighter bombers allowed 3 Air Fleet only to step up its number of fighter sorties from 156 to 378 the day after D-Day and 420 on 8 June, whence it gradually dropped to 34 on 19 June to rise again to 645 out of 709 sorties of all sorts on 30 June. The average daily number of fighter sorties was 366 in June and 346 in July. This improved the friend/foe ratio from 1.45 to 1.25, but did not change the situation.[35] Thirty-eight fighters got lost on average per day, totalling 1,040 up to 2 July.[36] About the same number of replacements were supplied in this period, which explains their unchanging weakness. None of Hitler's jet fighter-bombers swept over the beaches, and it was not before late July that a few flew some fighter-bomber missions in France.[37] As Colonel Priller, commander of Fighter Geschwader 26, wrote after the war, the German fighters were hunted.[38] Soon Air Fleet Reich ceased to return to the invasion front those fighter units that had been re-transferred home for refreshing and re-forming or re-equipping; it needed reinforcements itself. The Big Blow in the first critical hours of the invasion remained a dream.

III Flak Corps encountered other great difficulties when ordered in the afternoon of 6 June to proceed from the Somme–Scheldt area east of the Seine to the Caen area. The Seine bridges having been destroyed by bombing, it had to proceed via Paris and was not ready for combat in cooperation with Panzergruppe West before the morning of 9 June.[39] Had the Loire bridges been bombed earlier and not only just before and on D-Day, this would have indicated the actual invasion area and could have triggered a timely deployment of the Flak Corps in the right place.

Largely unmolested by German fighters, Allied interdiction operations before and after D-Day against roads, railroads and bridges proved very effective, as were the daytime strafing sweeps on troop columns and motor vehicle transports. They decisively reduced the mobility of the German armoured units, delayed their transfer from the interior of France to the battle front, and prevented their concentrated employment. The summer nights were too short for them to make up for the hours lost during daytime.

IInd Fliegerkorps, the only ground support command, depended entirely on the fighters of II Fighter Corps in attempting to penetrate the air umbrella to attack the enemy ground forces and invasion shipping, and such attacks soon became impossible. Moreover the fighter bomber pilots, having previously been home air defence pilots, had difficulties in adjusting to their new role because they had received no conversion training. Since the loss rate in fighter combat appeared to be 1:1 it was decided to abandon air battles, because equal loss figures meant very different things to the two sides considering the great disparities in numerical strength. As of 13 June, therefore, the main task of the fighters and fighter bombers was to protect the supply routes and the ground forces against Allied air power. Later, as of 1 July, II Fliegerkorps ceased to exist and was combined with II Fighter Corps, now commanded by General Bülowius, who replaced General Junck.[40] Meanwhile between 7 and 30 June the Allies bombed 117 airfields, which resulted in the loss of over 350 German aircraft on the ground. Moreover the bombing of German radar positions obscured the picture of the air situation in the minds of German staffs, and the rapid establishment of Allied airfields in the landing zone further aggravated the Luftwaffe situation. [41]

Not very much needs to be said about the German bomber forces, because on account of their numerical weakness and the lack of fighter cover they could not play an important role. Having to operate at night their success was small, and since the Germans were no longer accustomed to the presence of friendly aircraft at night, their anti-aircraft batteries frequently mistook them for enemy targets. Only 24 bombers could be mustered by IX Fliegerkorps on invasion day. Their radio guidance systems for new types of flying bombs became jammed.[42] After trying in vain to hit the Allied supply traffic across the Channel in the first days of the battle, the bombers switched over to mining the Seine estuary with new pressure mines. The Navy, however, fearing that its new mines would fall into the hands of the Allies, opposed and delayed such operations for about a week, by which time their possible effects were no longer important. As of 24 June some Mistal attacks were also attempted unsuccessfully. Notwithstanding gross exaggerations of German propaganda, few tangible results were achieved against Allied cross-Channel shipping. Bomber crew replacements were scant and rather inexperienced.

Later in July bombers were also used against enemy ground forces. 2 Flieger Division tried to operate at night and in bad weather with four torpedo bomber Gruppen from bases in southern France via intermediate airfields in central and eastern France. Their successes were negligible because of the lack of air reconnaissance and the destruction of the signal communications network. Only 30 to 40% of the He 177 long-range bombers of X Fliegerkorps were serviceable, but with full bomb load their ranges proved to be too short, which rendered them largely useless. Nevertheless German bombers raided London 12 times and Southampton three times during this period but these were merely nuisance raids. Up to 26 June the total Bomber strength in the west had fallen by 27% to 338 aircraft, of which only 200 were serviceable. These were less than 40% of the entire German bomber force, part of which was refreshing or converting in Germany; the largest part was fighting in Russia where the Soviets had started their big summer offensive in the centre of the eastern front on 22 June.[43]

The indiscriminate buzz bomb campaign was started by the Luftwaffe on 13 June with airborne-launching starting on 9 July, and on 7 September the Army began its V2 offensive. This offensive, however, lacked mass and was too inaccurate to accomplish much to the advantage of the German western front – apart from attracting a lot of bombs that would otherwise have been dropped on other German targets and from harassing the civilian population in Britain. On the contrary it triggered the Thunderclap operations. It is academic to comtemplate what the use of accurate flying bombs and rockets en masse against the invasion bases long before D-Day would have achieved.[44]

The USAAF resumption of the bombing attacks on oil in Germany 12 days after D-Day forced the Luftwaffe to shift its day fighters back and forth between the invasion and home fronts, but on 7 August it concentrated 300 fighters to support the tank thrust via Mortain towards Avranches in the attempt to cut off Patton's 3rd Army which had broken through and was about to encircle the nucleus of the German ground forces in the west near Falaise. Dornier Do 217 bombers with remote controlled gliding bombs had already tried to stop the American advance by attacking bridges, the full dimension of the breakthrough having been discovered on 2 August when, for the first time, a new Arado Ar 234 reconnaissance jet bomber succeeded in surveying the enemy side of the zone of operations.

Apart from its technological significance this feat shows how serious had been the absence of aerial reconnaissance for the Germans until then.[45] Just for completeness it should be mentioned that the Luftwaffe also engaged in supply flights to the ground troops defending the ports and fortresses along the north-western French coast.

By 1 July 1944 3 Air Fleet had flown about 14,000 sorties in the Normandy battle compared with 96,000 by the Allies.[46] By September it had almost completely withdrawn to Germany, where it was disbanded and replaced by Luftwaffenkommando West under Luftflotte Reich. The Western and home fronts had now merged in the air, partly also as a result of the invasion of southern France on 16

August. Meanwhile flight restrictions owing to lack of fuel were beginning to ground more and more bombers, with the bomber pilots being sent to training schools to become fighter pilots, and on 5 September these restrictions were extended to II Fighter Corps.[47] What Armament Minister Albert Speer had warned Hitler against in his second Hydration Memorandum of 28 July 1944[48] was beginning to become a reality: the Luftwaffe could well cease to operate in the foreseeable future. Having been unable to switch its efforts in time to air defence on account of Hitler's strategy and of the domination of offensive thought, it had now, after almost five years of incessant fighting, over-exerted itself; it could no longer fulfil its basic tasks and was bound to collapse.

Summing up, this much can be said:

1. The new air strategy – if it can be called so – introduced in late summer 1943 by General Korten, Jeschonnek's successor as Chief of the General Staff of the Luftwaffe, proved to be a failure by the spring of 1944. Its purpose had been to get away from the costly ground support operations which almost the entire Luftwaffe had engaged in with great losses on the major land fronts and to stress again the two basic strategic tasks: fighter defence and strategic bombing. The backbone of the German day-fighters was broken in spring 1944 by the American long-range escort fighters which achieved total air supremacy over Germany by day. Preparations for bombing the most important industrial centres of the Soviet Union along the Volga had to be abandoned on account of the receding front line and growing distances. Strategic bombing of Britain, the Baby Blitz, died of exhaustion in May 1944.

2. As a result the Luftwaffe was exhausted already in the months preceding the invasion and was unable to prepare for it to the extent it would have liked. There was no conversion training for fighter-bomber pilots, no common exercising between the ground support corps and army units, no familiarisation of reinforcement pilots with their assigned airfields, no anti-tank training of III Flakkorps, either because there was no time or because the relevant air fleets, in particular Air Fleet Reich, were so deeply engaged already that they could not spare the necessary personnel.

3. The invasion came as a tactical surprise, because unsatisfactory air reconnaissance, false intelligence and the wrong belief that the

main thrust would be in the Calais area (while other landings would be possible everywhere else) permitted no certainty about Allied plans and diffused the deployment of forces. The disadvantages of this, especially for the supply system and for the armoured troops, could not be redressed quickly enough on account of the overwhelming Allied air superiority.

4. All these shortcomings led to the disaster of the Luftwaffe's reinforcement transfers.

5. The Germans' newly introduced weapons did not yet function reliably, nor were enough available to turn their qualitative advantages into tactical and strategic success.

6. In this completely unequal situation it is difficult to say how the Luftwaffe leaders could have avoided mistakes or how else they could have acted in view of the pressures of the circumstances and the lack of satisfactory reconnaissance and intelligence.

7. While Hitler's ideological and psychological obduracy together with the Allied demand for unconditional surrender left no political option, the Luftwaffe in the west fought bravely until the bitter end.

8. The breakdown of German aviation fuel production after 12 May did not affect Luftwaffe operations immediately, because there were considerable stocks. Gradually, however, the bombers were put out of action and grounded, and then, beginning in September, flight restrictions were also imposed on fighter units. This initiated the final decline of the Luftwaffe.

9. Allied air supremacy was already seriously handicapping the Luftwaffe in the west before OVERLORD: it had to operate from bases too far away from the northern French coast to make optimum use of its aircraft. This air supremacy also impaired the mobility of the German ground and especially the armoured forces with all its consequences. The weakness in the air of the German Luftwaffe in the west, or, if one wants it, the almost total air supremacy of the Allies, was a decisive, if not *the* decisive element of the Allied victory in Normandy.

Notes

1 Horst Boog et al., Der Angriff auf die Sowjetunion (Stuttgart 1983) (= Vol. 4 of Das Deutsche Reich und der Zweite Weltkrieg, ed. Militärgeschichtliches Forschungsamt), p. 712.
2 Ibid., p. 697.
3 Goering and Saur, Chief of the Technical Department in Speer's Armament Ministry, on 23 May 1944, quoted in Alfred Price, The Last Year of the Luftwaffe, May 1944 to May 1945 (London, 1991), p. 13, 46.
4 Dieter Ose, Entscheidung im Westen 1944. Der Oberbefehlshaber West und die Abwehr der alliierten Invasion (Stuttgart 1982), p. 21 fn 3.
5 Directive No. 40 of 23 March 1942, in Walther Hubatsch (ed.) Hitler's Weisungen für die Kriegführung. Dokumente des Oberkommandos der Wehrmacht (München 1965), pp. 205–211.
6 Ose, op. cit., pp. 26 ff.; account of General Wolfgang Pickert, former Commanding General of III Flakkorps, Das III. Flakkorps in der Normandieschlacht (unpubl. manuscript of 20 April 1947), Militärgeschichtliches Forschungsamt (MGFA), Mil. Study No. B-597.
7 Ose, op. cit., pp. 47–60.
8 Ibid., pp. 57 ff.
9 Ibid., p. 219.
10 Michael Howard, Strategic Deception (London, 1990), (= Vol. 5 of British Intelligence in the Second World War, ed. Francis Harry Hinsley et al.), pp. 119–125, 131 f., 185–193, 198–200, and R.F. Hesketh, Fortitude. A History of Strategic Deception in North Western Europe, April 1943 to May 1945 (unpubl. manuscript of February 1949); Die Invasion im Spiegel der Funksprüche der Aufklärung der Luftflotte 3, der Funkhorchberichte der Marine etc., Bundesarchiv Militärarchiv Freiburg (BA-MA), RL 7/117, pp. 3, 6, 24, 30.
11 Directives Nos 51, 51a, 51b, and 51c of 3 Nov and 27 Dec 1943 and 17 Jan 1944, in Hitler's Weisungen, pp. 270–279.
12 Der Reichsmarschall des Grossdeutschen Reiches und Oberbefehlshaber der Luftwaffe, No. 8947/43 g.Kdos. Chefsache (Führungsstab Ia) of 6 Dec 1943, subject: Dr G. West, BA-MA RL 2/225.
13 Ibid. and Der Reichsmarschall des Grossdeutschen Reiches und Oberbefehlshaber der Luftwaffe No. 9050/44 g.Kdos. Chefs. (FüSt Ia) of 6 Jan 1944 and 2. Ang. of 7 Feb 1944, subject: Drohende Gefahr Nord; Oberbefehlshaber der Luftwaffe, Führungsstab Ia No. 9149/44 g.Kdos. Chefs. (op) of 4 Feb 1944 (re Portugal, Spain, Biscay); Oberbefehlshaber der Luftwaffe, Führungsstab Ia No. 9141/44 g.Kdos. Chefs. of 31 Jan 1944, subject: Drohende Gefahr Südost, all in BA-MA RL 2/225.
14 Der Reichsmarschall des Grossdeutschen Reiches und Oberbefehlshaber der Luftwaffe No. 9221/44 g.Kdos. Chefs. (FüSt Ia) of 27 Feb 1944, in BA-MA RL 2/225, and Karl Gundelach, "Drohende Gefahr West. Die Deutsche Luftwaffe vor und während der Invasion 1944", in Wehrwissenschaftliche Rundschau No. 6/1959, p. 301.

15 Gundelach, op. cit., p. 301.
16 Hans Speidel, Schlacht in der Normandie 1944. Führung, Gedanke und Ende des Feldmarschalls Rommel, unpubl. manuscript, MGFA Mil. Study C-017, p. 17.
17 Alfred Bülowius, Das II. Fliegerkorps an der Invasionsfront, Januar 1944 bis 13. Juni 1944. Unpubl. manuscript, MGFA Mil. Study No. B-620, pp. 6, 16.
18 Oberbefehlshaber der Luftwaffe, Führungsstab Ia/Chef NVW (Robinson) No. 8960/43 g.Kdos. Chefs. (op 1) of 11 Dec 1943, BA-MA RL 2/225; Gundelach, op. cit., p. 304. Erwin Notti, Flieger-Bodenorganisation in the Bretagne und Normandie, MGFA B-677.
19 Gundelach, op. cit., pp. 304, 307.
20 Josef Priller, Geschichte eines Jagdgeschwaders. Das Jagdgeschwader 26 (Schlageter) von 1937–1945 (Neckargemünd 1962).
21 Bülowius, op. cit., p. 6.
22 Pickert, op. cit., p. 6.
23 Gundelach, op. cit., p. 306.
24 Horst Boog, Die Deutsche Luftwaffenführung 1935–1945. Führungsprobleme, Spitzengliederung, Generalstabsausbildung (Stuttgart 1982), p. 30.
25 Williamson Murray, Strategy for Defeat. The Luftwaffe 1933–1945 (Air University Press Maxwell Alabama 1983), p. 240.
26 Boog, op. cit., p. 28 f.
27 Gundelach, op. cit., pp. 312–317; Walter Grabmann, Geschichte der Deutschen Luftverteidigung (unpubl. manuscript), MGFA Lw 11/b, pp. 686, 689; W. Gaul, Die Deutsche Luftwaffe während der Invasion 1944, in Wehrwissenschaftliche Rundschau, 1953, pp. 134 ff.
28 Bodo Zimmermann, Geschichte des Oberbefehlshabers West, Part A VII: Vor der Invasion, MGFA Mil. Study T-121, pp. 888–890. Interview of Generalleutnant Werner Junck, 19 May 1945, in: Library of Congress Washington, Spaatz Papers, Box 134; Gaul op. cit., pp. 135 f.; Gundelach, op. cit., p. 317, Price, op. cit., p. 6.
29 Gundelach, op. cit., pp. 317 f.; Adolf Galland, Die Ersten und die Letzten. Die Jagdflieger im Zweiten Weltkrieg (Darmstadt, 1953), pp. 299–318.
30 Gundelach, op. cit., p. 318; Wolfgang Birkenfeld, Der synthetische Treibstoff 1933–1945. Ein Beitrag zur nationalsozialistischen Wirtschafts- und Rüstungspolitik (Göttingen, 1964), pp. 172 ff., 228.
31 Luftwaffe Field Manual L.Dv. 16 "Luftkriegführung", par. 20.
32 MGFA Mil. Study T-121, Part B I, pp. 1,153 f. Nor could the U-Boats penetrate effectively to the invasion armada.
33 Gundelach, op. cit., pp. 318 f.; Grabmann, op. cit., pp. 754 ff.; Galland, op. cit., pp. 300–307; Alfred Price, The Last Year of the Luftwaffe. May 1944 to May 1945 (London, 1991), p. 58 ff.; Bülowius in MGFA Mil. Study B-620, pp. 32 ff.; Gaul, op. cit., pp. 140 ff.
34 Gundelach, op. cit., p. 319.
35 Ibid., pp. 319, 322; Grabmann, op. cit., pp. 834 ff.

36 MGFA Mil. Study T-121, Part B I, p. 1,155.
37 Price, op. cit., p. 61.
38 Priller, op. cit., pp. 232–249.
39 MGFA Mil. Study T-121, pp. 902, 1,103.
40 Kommandierender General II. Jagdkorps, Stabsbefehl No. 20 of 1 July 1944 in BA-MA RL 8/170; Gundelach, op. cit., p. 321.
41 Gaul, op. cit., p. 141; Gundelach, op. cit., pp. 321 ff.
42 Price, op. cit., pp. 58 f.; Gundelach, op. cit., p. 324; Gaul, op. cit., p. 145.
43 Price, op. cit., pp. 60 f.; Gaul, op. cit., pp. 143 f.; Gundelach, op.cit., pp. 324 ff.; Report 74 in BA-MA RL 8/65; MGFA Mil. Study B-509, p. 5
44 For the V-weapons and the British reaction see Public Record Office London PREM 3/89, 1412; CAB 65/42, 80/85; AIR 14/2732, 20/3227, 4837, 25/95; Heinz Dieter Hoelsken, Die V-Waffen. Entstehung, Propaganda, Kriegseinsatz (Stuttgart, 1984); Ralf Schabel, Die Illusion der Wunderwaffen. Düsenflugzeuge und Flugabwehrraketen in der Rüstungspolitik des Dritten Reiches (München, 1994); Basil Collier, The Defence of the United Kingdom (London, 1957).
45 Ose, op. cit., pp. 227 ff.; Gundelach, op. cit., p. 327; Price, op. cit., pp. 63 ff.
46 Gaul, op. cit., p. 142.
47 Gundelach, op. cit., p. 328; Price, op. cit., p. 65.
48 Birkenfeld, op. cit., p. 246.

Chairman

Dr Boog, you have given us a most illuminating analysis of the Luftwaffe situation and a catalogue of facts which explain very clearly how the gross imbalance of the opposing air forces came about.

To tell us as much as they can in the meagre 30 minutes or so now remaining our two joint speakers are going to take the stage again. They will cover the Normandy campaign itself, but will limit themselves to the period between D-Day and the end of the battle of the Falaise gap in August 1944.

January 1944 – Prime Minister Winston Churchill leaves Tunisia wearing the uniform of an Hon Air Commodore

Left to right: Lady Tedder, Squadron Officer Sarah Oliver (née Churchill), Air Chief Marshal Sir Arthur Tedder, Mrs Churchill and the Prime Minister

Flt Lt acting Squadron Leader Denis Crowley-Milling with his early Typhoon, familiary known as a Bombphoon before the advent of rockets, and with "Austin Seven" wind up windows. The bubble canopy came later.

General Dwight D Eisenhower Supreme Commander in front of D-Day map – dated 17th January 1944

Planning for D-Day, 1st February 1944
Left to right: Lieutenant General Omar N Bradley (American Forces), Admiral Sir B H Ramsey (Naval Forces), Air Chief Marshal Sir Arthur Tedder (Deputy Supreme Commander), General Dwight D Eisenhower (Supreme Commander), General Sir Bernard Montgomery (British Army), Air Chief Marshal Sir Trafford Leigh-Mallory (Air Commander-in-Chief) Lieutenant General W Bedell Smith (Chief of Staff)

D-Day minus – detailed PR coverage of a landing site

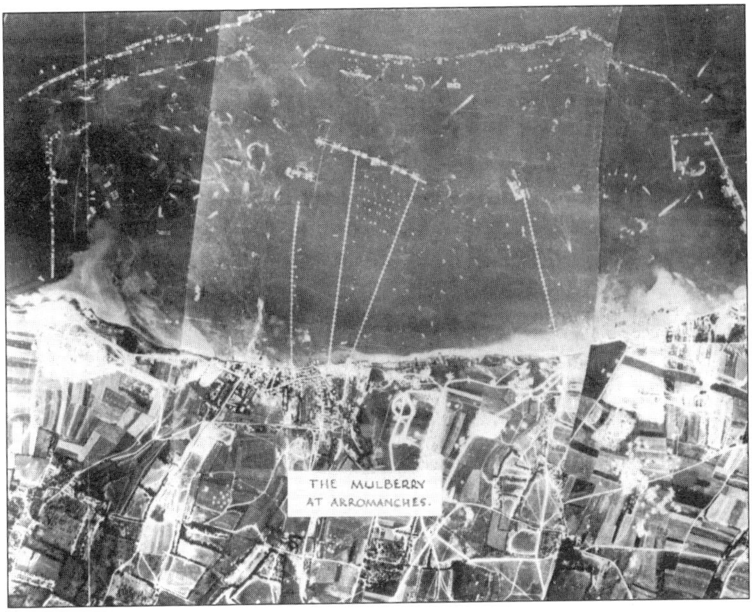
THE MULBERRY
AT ARROMANCHES.

A wider view

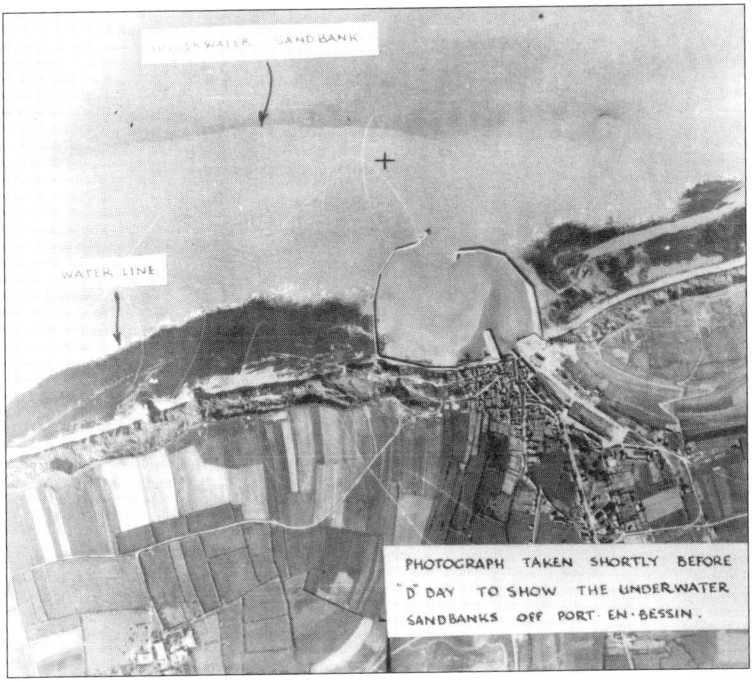
UNDERWATER SANDBANK
WATER LINE
PHOTOGRAPH TAKEN SHORTLY BEFORE
"D" DAY TO SHOW THE UNDERWATER
SANDBANKS OFF PORT-EN-BESSIN.

GLIDERS OF 6TH AIRBORNE DIVISION EAST OF R. ORNE
TAKEN BY SANDY WEBB ON "D" DAY.
INVASION ACTIVITY ON "D" DAY
SORTIE FLOWN BY A/CDRE.
GEDDES.

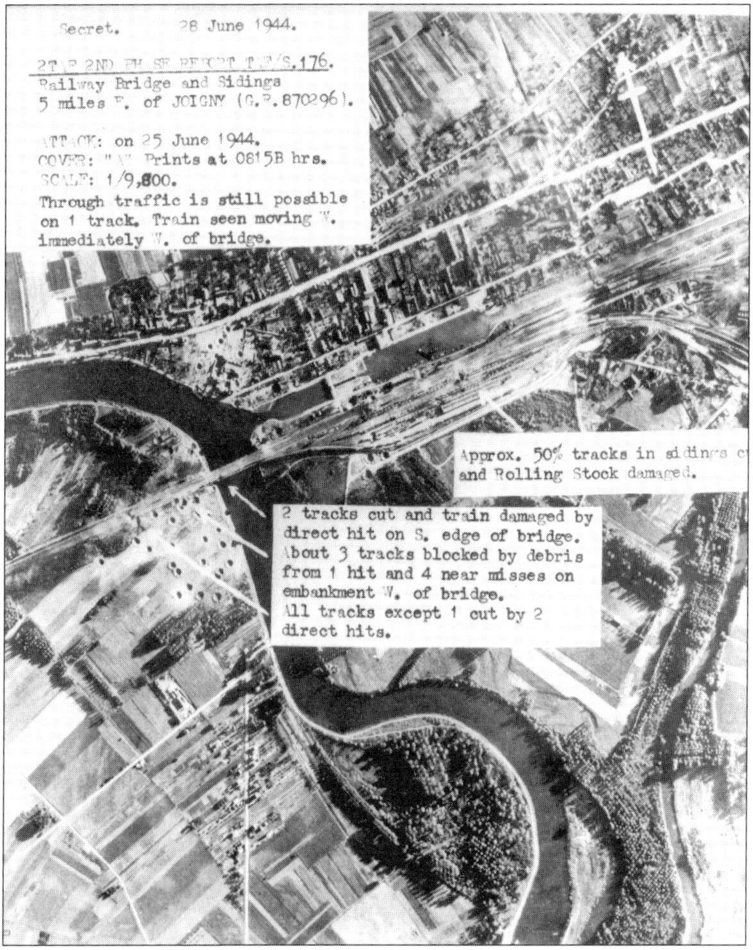
Secret. 28 June 1944.
Railway Bridge and Sidings
5 miles E. of JOIGNY (G.R.870296).
ATTACK: on 25 June 1944.
COVER: "A" Prints at 0815B hrs.
SCALE: 1/9,800.
Through traffic is still possible
on 1 track. Train seen moving W.
immediately W. of bridge.
Approx. 50% tracks in sidings
and Rolling Stock damaged.
2 tracks cut and train damaged by
direct hit on S. edge of bridge.
About 3 tracks blocked by debris
from 1 hit and 4 near misses on
embankment W. of bridge.
All tracks except 1 cut by 2
direct hits.

Group Captain J Fenton briefs Major C Gray of the "Queens" and Squadron Leader R A Sutherland at a Normandy visual contact point, 24th July 1944

Visual contact point in Normandy, July 1944, manned by the Royal Air Force and the Army

First WAAFs arrive in Normandy 6th August, 1944. Section Officer J Bradbury, Corporal Disney, LACW Davis and Sergeant Easson with recently liberated French civilians

Air Vice-Marshal Harry Broadhurst at an advanced airfield in Normandy, August 1944, with Marshal of the Royal Air Force Lord Trenchard, Group Captain P G Jameson (New Zealand) and Wing Commander R Johnston

Directing the "Cab Rank" overhead – an expression that was widely used but not strictly accurate. Aircraft were on "Offensive Patrol" but could be called on if required

Ops ordering aircraft airborne to support army in Normandy, August 1944

8. *The Overlord Campaign*

Lieutenant General Sir Napier Crookenden and Air Marshal Sir Denis Crowley-Milling

D C-M: Although the Allied Bomber offensive had not reduced German aircraft production, it had prevented its full realisation and had tied down in Germany massive resources in men and material for air defence. The Germans themselves reported that "the destruction of the Luftwaffe's ground organisation had been very effective, especially of the fighter airfields, hardly one of which was serviceable". The naval radar stations were mostly out of action and the Germans also recorded that "in the two months before D-Day nearly 1,900 aircraft were lost". Air supremacy had in fact been achieved by the combined and continuous efforts of the Allied Air Forces.

As to rail targets a report from the German Ministry of Transport on 3 June described the effect of the Allied air operations between March and June 1944: "The systematic destruction of all important junctions has seriously crippled the whole transport system, including railway installations and rolling stock. Paris is cut off from long-distance traffic and the most important bridges over the Seine have been destroyed."

In fact by dawn of D-Day the strategic forces alone had dropped over 66,000 tons on nearly eighty targets. The special duties squadrons at Tempsford continued to drop agents and explosives to French underground forces, who also took part in the destruction of bridges and rolling stock. As a result of all this, for example, 2nd SS Panzer Division took seventeen days to move from Toulouse to Normandy instead of the expected five.

At this point the Germans still remained doubtful as to where the blow would fall, and on the strength of the German met forecast on 4 June Rommel returned to Germany in the hope of seeing Hitler and explaining his urgent needs in the West and to celebrate his wife's birthday.

NC: More than that, the German Seventh Army, towards which the Allied invasion was steering, had ordered a war game at Rennes in

Brittany for all corps and divisional commanders to start at 9 am on 6 June. Only General Richter in the 716 Coastal Division and General Feuchtinger in 21 Panzer declined to attend.

At 0020 on 6 June five out of the six gliders detailed to attack the Orne bridges landed within fifty yards of the canal bridge, having released from their tugs at 5000 feet over Cabourg five miles to the north east. Complete surprise was achieved and the bridges were captured intact.

At 0050 hrs 3 Parachute Brigade suffered a very scattered drop due to the failure of the REBECCA/EUREKA pathfinder sets, the short flying time from the coast and the violent evasive action taken by some pilots on meeting flak over the coast. 5 Parachute Brigade had a better drop in reasonable concentration and in the evening lift at 2100 hrs, 246 gliders landed on the right landing zone out of 256 which had taken off.

The American 82nd and 101st were also given a very dispersed drop at the same time in the early morning – but both divisions were able to reach their objectives and their wide dispersion caused considerable confusion in the German command.

D C-M: The Bomber Command attacks on coastal batteries between midnight and 0500 hrs were generally successful and the bomb craters on many of them are still visible today. At St Martin de Varreville, one of the objectives of the 502nd Parachute Infantry of the 101st Airborne, the battery had been so heavily damaged before D-Day that the guns had been withdrawn and the position abandoned. The battery at Pointe du Hoc, now a US National Memorial to the US Rangers, was captured by a remarkable cliff assault, only to find no guns, some heavily damaged casemates and a resolute and hard fighting garrison.

Overlooking the landing beaches of the British 50th Division was the Longues Battery. On D-Day the battery was active and was engaged by HMS *Ajax* at 0530 hrs, but just before 0600 hrs the battery opened fire again on the Headquarters ship HMS *Bulolo*, forcing her to move. The battery was finally silenced by the fire of HMS *Ajax* and *Argonaut*. The Mont Fleury Battery never opened fire and when the Green Howards reached it at about 0800, they found a very shaken and dispirited lot of gunners, who were only too glad to surrender. The last of these batteries in the assault area was Merville. Attacked by a hundred Lancasters at 0030 hrs the battery was damaged and cratered, but none of the casemates were penetrated and only two were hit. Most of the bombs fell to the south of the battery. But this battery too was silenced.

So the massive Allied convoys crossed the Channel and landed their troops without enemy air opposition, thanks to the combined efforts of the Allied Air Forces in reducing the fire of the enemy ground forces holding the beaches, except on OMAHA Beach, where the bombing, and also the naval gunfire, fell beyond the beach defences, leaving them generally intact. That, with the loss of most of the American swimming tanks in choppy seas, made OMAHA a near disaster.

NC: The British 3rd Division landed on SWORD Beach without major difficulty and the assault brigade had reached the Perier Ridge three miles inland by 0900 hrs. The reserve brigade and the tanks of the Staffordshire Yeomanry were held up by the fighting ahead of them and by congestion on the beach and in the narrow beach exits. The Division's task was to capture Caen that evening, but by 1900 hrs they were held up three miles short of the city by the arrival of 21 Panzer Division.

In the centre of the British sector the 3rd Canadian Division, landing astride Courseulles, met considerable fire on the beaches, but by 1430 hrs they were five miles inland and two troops of tanks had reached the Caen-Bayeux road.

On the right the British 50th Division landed on GOLD Beach and by the evening of D-Day they had cleared Arromanches and were in the outskirts of Bayeux.

At OMAHA the assault craft of the US 1st and 29th Divisions were met by intense machine gun, mortar and artillery fire from the German defences on the dunes above the beach and for some time the survivors, crouched under the sea wall, could make little movement forward. Then some determined leadership from a few officers and men got them moving and by nightfall their lodgement was secure. In contrast the American VII Corps, landing at UTAH on the east shore of the Cherbourg Peninsula, suffered only 147 casualties and soon made contact with the 101st Airborne inland. Both air and sea bombardment had been accurate and effective.

D C-M: Through the day's fighting air reconnaissance had reported the movement through Caen of 21 Panzer Division and the approach of 12 SS and Panzer Lehr Panzer Divisions from the Chartres area. Typhoons had already scored six tanks in the northern suburbs of Caen.

The Allied air forces were engaged all day in providing continuous air cover for the mass of shipping in the Channel, and in giving tactical air support to the armies. 2 TAF put up 2,000 sorties, in fairly poor weather conditions, while 3,000 sorties from the Ninth Air Force carried out similar tasks for the American First Army. A thousand

Bomber Command aircraft attacked road and rail targets in an arc from Paris to Carentan, losing twelve aircraft in the process, while Mosquitos and Mitchells from 2 TAF struck at targets on the roads from Falaise and Villers Bocage. Next day 330 heavy bombers attacked the Paris Ceinture railway system, twenty-nine were lost, and for the next three days similar and continuous air operations took place. The RAF Servicing Commandos and 4 RE airfield construction wings were put ashore on 7 June.

NC: By the end of the first three days the 3rd British and 3rd Canadian Divisions were held up in heavy fighting north of Caen by three German Panzer Divisions; 50th Division was now well south of the Caen–Bayeux road; and the Americans were fighting to join up their two bridgeheads at Carentan. Montgomery was well aware of the urgent need to capture Caen, to expand the bridgehead and to make more room for airfields, and he now decided to achieve these aims by two encircling attacks round Caen from the east and from the west.

51st (H) Division were to attack east of Caen and 7th Armoured Division were to drive through Villers Bocage to the high ground round Evrecy. The British 1st Airborne Division was to drop south of Caen to fill the gap between these two prongs.

D C-M: Leigh-Mallory objected to this plan on the grounds that the 1st Airborne Division could not be landed in sufficient strength and that the Navy would give no guarantee of not firing on the 38 and 46 Group aircraft by day or by night. General Urquhart and Air Marshal Hollinghurst began planning, but the airborne plan was finally dropped – happily for the men of the 1st Airborne Division, since both ground attacks from east and west failed.

NC: The attack by the 51st Highland Division east of Caen failed and the advance of the 7th Armoured Division west of the city was held up by elements of 12 SS Panzer and Panzer Lehr. After two days of bitter tank and infantry fighting, the division tried a left hook, made good progress through Villers Bocage, but then ran into Major Witman's 501st Heavy Tank Company. In five minutes of violent action, five German Tiger tanks destroyed twenty-five British Shermans, captured the commanding officer of the leading armoured regiment and drove 7th Armoured out of Villers Bocage.

A major factor affecting the whole campaign was the power of the German Tiger and Panther tanks. The Sherman and the Cromwell in the British, Canadian and American armies were mechanically more reliable, but their 75mm gun was outranged and outmatched by the German long 75mm in the Panther and the 88mm in the Tiger and in their anti-tank batteries. In Normandy only one Sherman in four now had the British 17-pounder gun, which could knock out a Tiger, if struck in the right place, but the Allied tank crews went into action knowing that a Panther or a Tiger could knock them out at long range – and that their Sherman might well flame.

On 18 June a storm blew up, destroyed the American Mulberry Harbour and damaged the British one. The build-up of 21 Army Group was delayed and only on 23 June were Second Army and 83 Group able to launch a second attempt to break through west of Caen. This time three infantry divisions fought their way forward for five miles and the 11th Armoured succeeded in crossing the Odon River and engaging in a furious battle for Hill 112.

VIII Corps were now in a salient five miles deep and only two miles wide. Attempts to widen it failed and 9th and 10th SS Panzer Divisions had now arrived. Five panzer divisions were now facing Second Army and General Dempsey decided to consolidate on the line of the River Odon.

D C-M: Throughout both these hard-fought battles 2 TAF had provided tactical support and close armed reconnaissance over the battlefield. Forty Typhoons of 83 Group and sixty-one Mitchells of 2 Group found and attacked the headquarters of Panzer Group West near Thury Harcourt, saturated the orchard, where most of the vehicles were concealed, killed General von Dawans, the Chief of Staff, and seventeen other officers, and put the headquarters completely out of action.

Two days later eleven squadrons of 2 TAF attacked Tilly sur Seulles, Senaudiers and Lingevres with bombs, rockets and cannon, supported by 300 aircraft of Bomber Command covering the withdrawal of 7th Armoured. At this point, 14 June, Coningham, supported by Tedder, announced at the daily AEAF conference in England that the withdrawal was a severe setback and that the situation "had the makings of a dangerous crisis". Leigh-Mallory flew over to visit Montgomery that same afternoon, taking Montgomery's Chief of Staff (De Guingand) with him, and on the 16th Coningham reminded the Army where they had planned to be on D+10 and suggested that they admit that the plan had failed.

NC: Neither Montgomery, nor any other soldier, felt that there had been any sort of crisis and the Army representatives at the AEAF conference had said so loudly and clearly. Montgomery and Leigh-Mallory discussed the whole situation and the future support of the Army by both medium and heavy bombers and parted on much improved terms.

D C-M: Air reconnaissance on 20 June had confirmed that 1 SS

Panzer was moving from Belgium, but heavy and medium bomber attacks on railways in Belgium, in the Mantes-Orleans gap and at Paris, Chartres and Dreux so delayed the Division's move that it was not fully complete in the battle until 9 July.

For much of the three days of this second attack west of Caen bad weather prevented flying from England, but 83 Group flew a large number of sorties and shot down twenty-six German fighters, making one of their rare appearances. In the intervals of fair weather Mosquitos and Mitchells from 2 TAF bombed enemy troops by day and by night using flares.

It was on 27 June that Montgomery wrote to the CIGS, General Brooke, expressing his view that Coningham was a "bad man, not genuine and terribly jealous . . . spends his time trying to trip up Leigh-Mallory" – a letter symptomatic of the poor relations between Montgomery, Tedder and Coningham and only rivalled by Tedder's letter the following month to Eisenhower, copied to the Chief of the Air Staff, suggesting the removal of Montgomery.

NC: The German defences around the north of Caen had by now been greatly strengthened with three belts of anti-tank ditches and mine fields and a chain of fortified villages.

Three divisions now attacked the city – 3rd British on the left, 59th British in the centre in their first battle and 3rd Canadian on the right, supported by two Canadian armoured brigades and the specialised tanks of 79th Armoured and massive artillery and naval gunfire support.

D C-M: For the first time Bomber Command operated in close support of ground forces and the bomb line was therefore set 6,000 yards ahead of the leading troops. As a result the bombers' attack went in the evening before and the bombs fell on the enemy's rear defences behind the main German defended localities. H-Hour for the ground assault was at 0420 hrs the next morning.

The use of heavy bombers in this way was strongly opposed by Coningham, as he maintained that it would produce so many craters and so much rubble that the Army's advance would be hindered – and so it proved. In fact 450 Halifaxes and Lancasters flew in at low altitude from the north with a Spitfire escort and dropped over 2,000 tons. Caen disappeared in a great cloud of smoke and dust, lit by the flashes of the exploding bombs. Soon after 0700 hrs next morning 250 medium bombers of the 9th Air Force attacked strong points, gun areas, bridges and headquarters, and fighter bombers of 2 TAF ranged further afield on the approaches to the city.

NC: By the evening of 10 July the 3rd British and 3rd Canadian

Divisions had met on the banks of the Orne and Caen was finally in our hands. It had been a costly affair – 350 casualties and the loss of eighty tanks. For the next three days pressure on the German forces on both sides of Caen was kept up and in another savage battle for Hill 112 the German Tiger tank company which had damaged 7th Armoured Division three weeks before was finally destroyed.

Bradley's First Army was now fighting hard to reach St Lo and to prepare for their break-out battle, Operation COBRA. Montgomery and his two Army commanders, Dempsey and Bradley, were still in full accord on the strategy of drawing the German armour onto the British in the east, so facilitating Bradley's break-out to the south and west.

D C-M: On 13 July Montgomery signalled Eisenhower, asking for full air support for two major attacks – Operation GOODWOOD by the British VIII Corps with three armoured divisions, east of the Orne on 18 July, and COBRA by the American First Army near St Lo on 19 July. Eisenhower's enthusiastic reply made it clear that he had misunderstood Montgomery's intention and now regarded Bradley's attack as helping Second Army – a complete reversal of the facts.

To confuse things further at SHAEF Montgomery signalled Tedder, emphasizing the importance of the air role with the words "the plan promises to be decisive". Naturally Tedder took this to mean that Second Army's armoured attack in the east was intended to be a break-out operation, whereas Montgomery claimed that "decisive" referred to the whole plan – British and American.

NC: The limited nature of Montgomery's aims for Second Army were made plain in his directive to Dempsey on 15 July. He was to "write down" the German armour, gain a good bridgehead over the Orne, improve our position on the eastern front and destroy German equipment and personnel. From 15 to 17 July XII and the Canadian Corps, with full air support, attacked the enemy west of Caen in more hard fighting and in England Eisenhower, Tedder, Leigh-Mallory, Coningham and the Americans now all agreed that a massive programme of air support would be laid on for both GOODWOOD and COBRA.

D C-M: On 15 and 16 July Rommel toured the area east of Caen and warned his commanders that the British would attack in that area within the next two days. Next day, 17 July, he drove to Sepp Dietrich's Panzer Corps headquarters, but as his car reached the main road near Vimoutiers, the air sentry, Corporal Holke, sitting in the back of the car, yelled that there were two aircraft coming in fast and low from the rear. He was too late. The aircraft opened fire, the driver was killed, the car went out of control into the ditch and Rommel was badly wounded in the head. It was his last day in action. The damage was done by Typhoon pilots from 193 Squadron, 84 Group; at this stage they were scouring the roads, looking for anything to shoot up – but little expecting to bag a Field Marshal.

The air support plan for GOODWOOD provided for Bomber Command to attack the enemy defended areas on the flanks of the armoured divisions' thrust line, including the fortified villages of Touffreville, Sannerville, Banneville, and Manneville, with 1,000 and 500 bombs and the strongly defended village of Cagny in the path of the advance with bombs with instantaneous fuses. Heavy bombers of the 8th Air Force were to bomb one area just west of Troarn and two more targets to the south of the armoured objectives, where much of the enemy's artillery had been located. Mediums of the 9th Air Force would attack enemy forward positions, pre-selected gun positions and strong points during the battle and would provide continuous support through the ASSU tentacles. Over 4,500 aircraft would take part in the battle, dropping 7,700 tons. It would be the heaviest and most concentrated air attack in daylight ever attempted in support of ground forces.

NC: At 0530 hrs on 18 July the artillery opened fire on the German flank defences and for the next 45 minutes a thousand Lancasters and Halifaxes bombed their targets. As they finished, the monitor *Roberts* and the cruisers *Mauritius* and *Enterprise* shelled enemy positions. At 0700 hrs 9th Air Force mediums found many of their targets obscured by smoke and dust and at 0830 hrs 8th Air Force Liberators began their attacks further south. The Bomber Command targets on the flanks were well covered and the Germans there were so shocked by the weight of the bombing that they offered little resistance. In Cagny, however, German tanks and 88mm guns held out for most of the day, led by Colonel von Luck, and the village was only cleared by the Guards Armoured Division that evening.

By nightfall 11th Armoured had reached the second railway line, but could get no further, after beating off two German counter-attacks. Behind them traffic jams had begun to build up and 7th Armoured Division could only get into action next day. On the left Guards Armoured ran into the 503rd Heavy Tank Company, led by Leutnant von Rosen. Both von Luck and Rosen later spent many years telling us all about it on the Army Staff College battlefield tours.

By now the high ground of the Bourgebus ridge had been reinforced by elements of 1st, 12th SS and 21 Panzers and the next day saw more heavy fighting. Little progress was made and Montgomery decided to consolidate the ground gained. Although GOODWOOD had achieved the aim of holding the German armour in the east and deepening the bridgehead east of Caen, the Germans had not been as badly mauled as had been hoped, we had lost 200 tanks and there was no break through.

D C-M: This limited success caused disappointment at SHAEF and in the UK and US. Matters were made worse by the wording of the official communiqué issued by 21 Army Group in the evening of 18 July – "early this morning British and Canadian troops of Second Army attacked and broke through into the areas east of the Orne and south east of Caen . . . strong armoured and mobile forces are operating in open country farther to the south east and south". Both SHAEF and the press took this to mean a break through into undefended country.

NC: Eisenhower visited Montgomery on 20 July, as the battle ended, and once again Montgomery explained the close relationship of GOODWOOD to COBRA, the drive through St Lo. Yet Eisenhower's subsequent letter to Montgomery showed that he had still not appreciated the continuous pressure maintained by Second Army along most of its front, or the fact that only one, much weakened Panzer division, Panzer Lehr, had moved to the American front, while four new German infantry divisions had reinforced the seven battered Panzer divisions still opposite the British.

D C-M: In the meantime bad weather had intervened and the main 8th Air Force attack had been postponed to 24 July and then again to the 25th. Sadly, some B-17s never received the recall and dropped their bombs on the 24th, some of them on American troops. Next day at 0940 hrs some 600 fighter-bombers from the 9th Air Force opened the attack, followed by 150 heavies, again with some bombs falling short.

NC: General Collins' VII Corps advanced and after two days fighting broke through the main German defences. Two days later they were in Coutances and the German withdrawal began to look more and more like a rout. During the next six days the Canadian Corps with 7th and Guards Armoured Divisions attacked southwards down the Falaise Road, supported by 1,700 2 TAF sorties, and XXX and VIII Corps drove southwards from Caumont, keeping up the pressure on the German armour.

D C-M: On 5 August Coningham finally moved his main headquarters from Uxbridge to alongside Montgomery's at Le Tranquay, south of Bayeux. By 7 August American forces had reached Mayenne and Laval when, on Hitler's personal order four Panzer divisions, 116th, 1st and 2nd SS and 2nd, counter-attacked Mortain on the left flank of the American advance. The German armour was only just held by the 30th and 9th Divisions, but a brief warning from ULTRA the previous evening allowed Broadhurst and Quesada to concert the air effort of 83 Group and the 9th Air Force.

On the morning of the 7th the weather was foul, everything dripping wet, and no signs of a break. Eventually a weather recce took off from 121 Wing, 83 Group, flying south west, crossing the American sector and making a wide sweep around Avranches above the overcast. Suddenly a hole appeared in the cloud and they dived down almost to the deck – and there, on the outskirts of Mortain, were what seemed like hundreds of German tanks. The weather started to break up and the 'Day of the Typhoon' was about to begin.

The momentum of 1st Panzer Division was soon brought to a crawl. The air was full of aircraft, diving from various directions and at all angles amidst a barrage of light ack-ack. Some were shot down and, sadly, there were some mid-air collisions. Wave after wave, back to the airstrip and refuel. It went on until 4 o'clock in the afternoon – some squadrons doing three or four sorties.

NC: On the same day General Guy Simonds launched his II Canadian Corps, the 51st Division and the Polish Armoured Division down the Falaise road. They were preceded by over a thousand Bomber Command aircraft – for the first time attacking targets by night ahead of tanks and infantry riding in armoured personnel carriers. The exploding bombs, and the mass of moving vehicles produced a blinding cloud of smoke and dust, so obscuring the targets that a third of the bombers returned to base with their bombs.

D C-M: The advance went well and next day Typhoons, Spitfires and Mustangs ranged over the battlefield, attacking opportunity targets. At midday the Polish Armoured Division started to drive for Falaise and the 8th Air Force took over at short notice from Bomber Command. Heavy flak caused them a number of casualties and although the sky was now clear only 500 of the 678 aircraft released their bombs – many of which fell wide, causing 300 casualties among British, Canadian and Polish troops.

NC: Patton's 3rd Army had by now turned eastwards. On 8 August Montgomery and Bradley agreed that XV Corps on the left of Patton's drive should turn to the north and capture Alençon, so narrowing the only escape route for the German 7th Army. Bradley believed that the German armour was already sluicing back through the gap and ordered his troops to go no further north – "rather a hard shoulder there, than a broken back in the gap". On the 14th First Canadian Army resumed their drive for Falaise with the support of medium bombers from 2 TAF and 8,700 aircraft of Bomber Command. Most of them were on target, but seventy-seven dropped short and there were some 500 Canadian casualties.

D C-M: Next day the new German C-in-C, Kluge, was shot up by Allied fighter bombers. Hitler replaced him with Model, who now ordered all German units to move eastwards. Remnants of 2nd, 9th and 12 SS and 21 Panzer together with the 3rd Parachute Division fought desperately to hold open the Falaise Gap, but the Allied air forces got to work in what was to be the best demonstration of the tactical use of air power. Between 16 and 21 August Mitchells, Mosquitos, Typhoons, Mustangs, Spitfires and P-47s caused utter destruction to the massed columns of German tanks, trucks and men on their feet, struggling to move eastwards. The Falaise Gap was never fully closed and 20,000 Germans got away to fight another day, but the Allies took 50,000 prisoners. Within the area of the Falaise Gap an Operational Research Group counted 344 tanks and self-propelled guns, 2,447 trucks and cars and 252 towed guns. Out of the 2,500 German tanks and assault guns committed to Normandy, only 120 got back over the Seine.

NC: 21 Army Group and 2 TAF now set off on their gallop to Brussels. Patton's 3rd Army approached Paris, Eisenhower took command in the field and the arguments began about a single, concentrated thrust to the Rühr or an advance on a broad front – but that is another story.

Chairman

Many thanks for that very clear account of the actual campaign, bringing together all the threads introduced by the previous speakers.

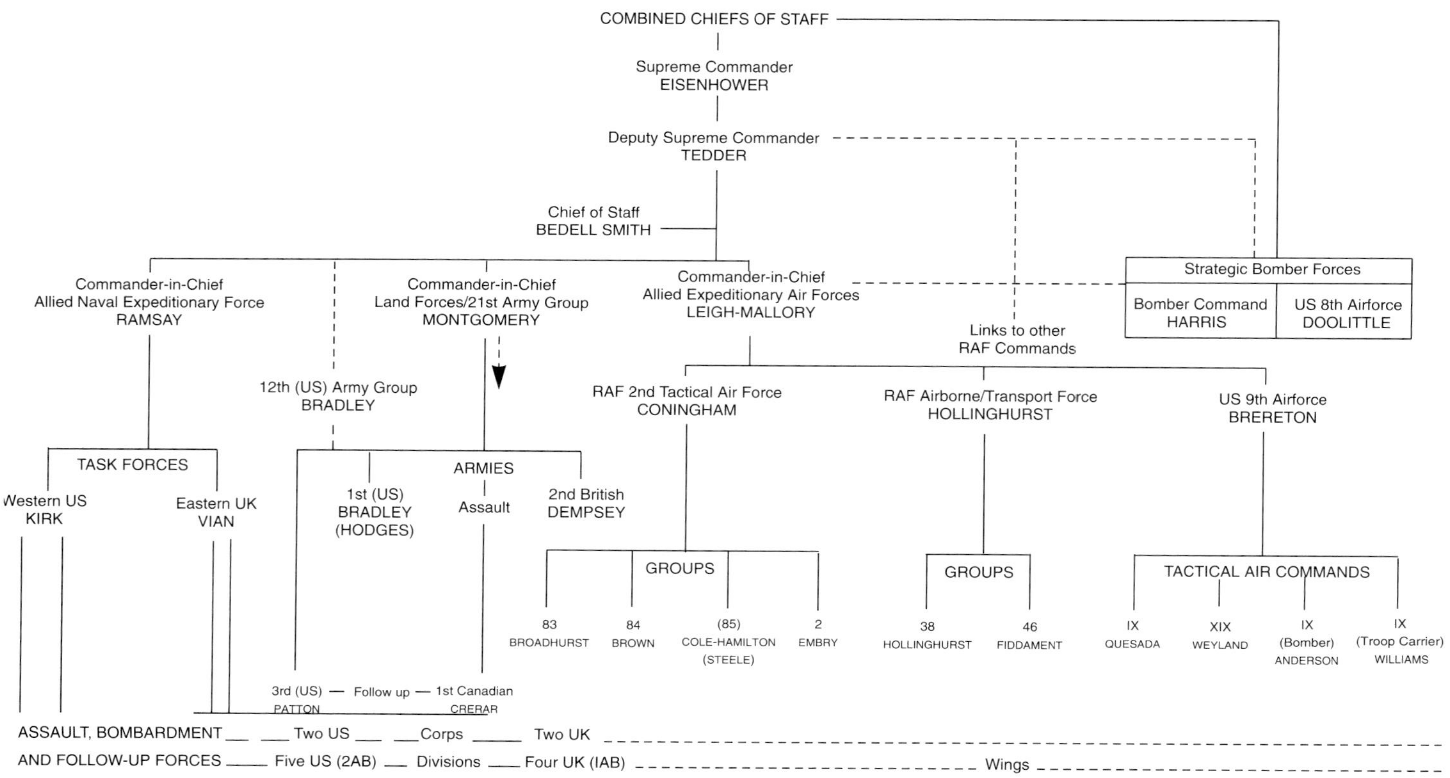
COMBINED CHIEFS OF STAFF
Supreme Commander
EISENHOWER
Deputy Supreme Commander
TEDDER
Chief of Staff
BEDELL SMITH
Strategic Bomber Forces
Bomber Command
HARRIS
US 8th Airforce
DOOLITTLE
Commander-in-Chief
Allied Naval Expeditionary Force
RAMSAY
Commander-in-Chief
Land Forces/21st Army Group
MONTGOMERY
Commander-in-Chief
Allied Expeditionary Air Forces
LEIGH-MALLORY
Links to other
RAF Commands
12th (US) Army Group
BRADLEY
RAF 2nd Tactical Air Force
CONINGHAM
RAF Airborne/Transport Force
HOLLINGHURST
US 9th Airforce
BRERETON
TASK FORCES
Western US
KIRK
Eastern UK
VIAN
ARMIES
1st (US)
BRADLEY
(HODGES)
Assault
2nd British
DEMPSEY
GROUPS
83
BROADHURST
84
BROWN
(85)
COLE-HAMILTON
(STEELE)
2
EMBRY
GROUPS
38
HOLLINGHURST
46
FIDDAMENT
TACTICAL AIR COMMANDS
IX
QUESADA
XIX
WEYLAND
IX
(Bomber)
ANDERSON
IX
(Troop Carrier)
WILLIAMS
3rd (US) — Follow up — 1st Canadian
PATTON
CRERAR
ASSAULT, BOMBARDMENT
AND FOLLOW-UP FORCES
Two US
Five US (2AB)
Corps
Divisions
Two UK
Four UK (IAB)
Wings

9. *Digest of Group Discussions*

Strategic Considerations

Among strategic issues was the necessity for OVERLORD; could not the combined bombing offensive have won the war on its own, some wondered. *Lord Bramall*, while regarding the bomber offensive as essential to victory, had no doubts. To bring that very, very tough nation Germany to its knees and satisfy our Allies that we were doing everything possible we would have had to bomb every single town in Germany until they collapsed. The bomber offensive and getting armies into Germany were complementary. Both were necessary to win the war. Until our armies were back on the Continent ready to move in a direct line to Germany we could not be certain; Hitler would have had time to stabilise the Eastern Front and rebuild his war machine. He had very many people with ingenuity. He could have used his V1 and V2 offensive. He might have found the secret of the atomic bomb. The two were vital. If you were landing on the Continent, it had to be just near enough to permit air cover, which was absolutely essential, yet far enough away to make their interior lines of communication that much more difficult. The Normandy route had a much better chance of success than the Pas de Calais, where counter-attack could come much quicker. "If we had to have an army on the Continent, and I think we did, I do not think we had much chance of improving on the OVERLORD strategy."

Dr Boog was of similar opinion. Had the invasion not occurred, the war would have dragged on, for the Germans were relocating their industry underground and far from the main bombing effort. He did not think the war would have been ended purely by strategic bombing; the dropping of an atomic bomb would have been the only way of ending it quickly. *Sir Michael Beetham* thought timing an important factor. Had the Germans not experienced technical problems with the jet fighter, then the outcome of the bomber offensive might have been different. He wondered also what the Allies would have done had they developed the atomic bomb earlier; what would Churchill and Roosevelt have done? *Dr Boog* observed that a question so far overlooked by Second World War historiography had been raised by an American historian, Sherry, namely the racial prejudice affecting American decision making. He had suggested that the Americans had little difficulty in deciding to go ahead with the dropping of the atomic weapon against the Japanese, simply because the Americans viewed the Japanese as inferior. This was an historical "if", but it would have been interesting to see whether the Americans could have used an atomic weapon against Germany. *Sir Michael Beetham* responded that there would also have been practical problems involved in using such a weapon against Germany, and perhaps Churchill and Roosevelt were mindful of these. Given the proximity of Britain to Germany, the Allies would have had to consider the consequences of fall-out from an atomic weapon, ensuring first that the wind was blowing in the right direction. These considerations would have limited the "atomic option" in the west, and there would have been more agonising over the decision to use the weapon against Germany.

Few doubted that OVERLORD was essential, and critical to its success was air supremacy, achieved over the preceding months. For *Charles Messenger* the key moment came in February 1944. Until then, the P-51 fighters escorting the USAAF bombers over Germany had been ordered to stick with the bombers; then they were told not to worry about the bombers any more but to go out and get the Luftwaffe. That was when air superiority started to move towards air supremacy. *Lord Bramall*, who believed the whole campaign had been a fairly close-run thing, paid tribute too to the interdiction programme and air bombardment, without which "there was no way we were going to (a) get ashore, (b) fight off counter-attacks, and (c) break out and destroy the enemy. With no better than air parity, the losses of the invasion fleet would have been very considerable. We put 156,000 men in on the first day, 10,000 of whom were killed or wounded, and that with complete air superiority. Without it OVERLORD would have failed and the war could have gone on indefinitely. It was absolutely essential in an operation like that to have won the air battle first."

Nevertheless there had certainly been much political in-fighting over the use of one of the essential elements of air power to support the invasion, namely the heavy bombers, and *Mr Cox* commented that for those taking the decisions the situation was not as simple as it appeared today. Not only were there powerful competing personalities, but other factors were also in competition. *Dr Boog* had described the effect of bombing on German oil production, and *Sir Napier*

Crookenden and *Sir Denis Crowley-Milling* had described its effect on the French rail network. Both target systems were vulnerable to the strategic bombers, and both could potentially cripple any German response to OVERLORD. It was plainly desirable to bomb German oil, but Leigh-Mallory was constantly concerned because he believed the 8th Air Force wished to bomb oil targets in Germany to the detriment of attacks he wished them to mount in France – in fact he complained far more in this respect about the 8th Air Force than he did about Bomber Command. But it was not simply a question of halting attacks on Germany, because other potential consequences might have followed. First, there would probably have been a transfer of German fighters from the Reich, which, as *Dr Boog* had pointed out, was planned but never happened, with subsequent implications for air superiority. Second, oil production would have recovered to some extent with positive effects for German ground and air operations. Moreover there were understandable political sensitivities over the transportation plan, and the level of casualties predicted amongst the friendly French civilians ran into tens of thousands. The political hesitations therefore became understandable, especially since the campaign was supposed to be one of liberation, and the views of French resistance and Free French forces had to be taken into account – De Gaulle never being an easy man to deal with at the best of times. The decision was finally made after an operational experiment, ie the six raids on marshalling yards by Bomber Command, had proved that casualties would actually be much lower, though they ran into the hundreds on some raids.

Lieutenant Colonel Lacey-Johnson, author of a book on Normandy, was sure that the heavy bombers were essential. Solly Zuckerman, the architect of this plan, always contended that the problem was strategic rather than tactical; it was thanks to his getting it adopted in that way and using the heavy bombers on it that it worked. If the opposers of his plan had had their way and left the bombing to the very last moment it could not have been successful. In the event what really caused the demise of the French railways was not so much the cutting of railway lines or the knocking out of rolling stock, but the lack of servicing of locomotives; it was that which finally brought them to a halt. The prime object of the transportation plan, he went on, was to delay the arrival of the tanks and it was they that suffered. A lot of the German units got there, but without their tanks.

As *Group Captain Verity* pointed out, the RAF contributed to this in a further way, through its support of the French resistance and other undercover organisations in occupied Europe. He was in charge of the

SOE air operations room for the first six months of 1944, and on any one night it was not unusual to see a hundred bomber aircraft allocated to drops for the Maquis alone, not to mention the remainder of occupied Europe. Drops would include canisters of weapons, agents and wireless operators. As a result in the six months prior to D-Day, a thousand locomotives were put out of action, and this was when the bombers were not operating at full potential. When they got the 'green light' the night before D-Day, 950 rail cuts were made, and 380 telecommunications lines were cut. As a consequence of the latter, the Germans could not use land-line communications so effectively, and had to rely on W/T and radio, which could be intercepted more easily by the Allies. *Sir Napier Crookenden* commented on the consequences of such activities, saying that the Army was greatly helped by the holding back of the German armour during the crucial period. The enemy had wanted to do this so as to defeat the Allies in a battle of manoeuvre, ignoring the fact that they could not manoeuvre in face of air superiority (and all the other impediments placed in their way).

Security and Deception

Lord Craig, who as Chief of the Defence Staff had been involved in setting up the Gulf War, referred to the amount of notice needed to start the operation. "We had had a period of sanctions and preparations before the decision to go, and it was very important to know how much warning we should have. It was fairly straightforward in that this was an air campaign where we did not need all that much warning once we were ready to go. D-Day in Normandy, on the other hand, which was delayed by one day, involved every conceivable type of ship, unit, aircraft – in every kind of role. Then there were the problems of security – does anyone have experience of whether that delay caused difficulties? Were they even aware of the delay?" *Mr Peter Rudd*, a pilot with 605 Squadron, intruding with Mosquito Mark VIs and operating from Manston, replied "I flew on the night of D-Day and the next two nights and my main recollection is about the weather. We knew nothing about the postponement – we went to the airfield for briefing on the afternoon of the 5th to do our night flying tests and still knew nothing. It was only later, when we got airborne and saw the shipping, that we realised it was happening. There were so many ships we could have walked across! We were not aware it had been postponed, and only when we landed did we realise it was actually on for that night, and we were confined to camp. Reading from my log-book it says for the night 5/6 'weather not so good in patches; cloud 10/10ths in places' – remember we had no navigation aids, it was all map reading and visual recognition – 'weather poor en route, 10/10ths, rain nearly the whole way'. On the third night, returning from Chartres, cloud was 10/10ths at 1,000 ft. This sort of thing continued through June, as we heard this morning. But for the invasion we would not have flown. The cloud was 800 ft at Manston, which was like Piccadilly Circus when we came back."

Group Captain Richardson commented that with the whole of southern England crammed full of transport, guns, ammunition dumps and the uniformed personnel milling around, it would have been impossible to deceive the Germans about the imminence of invasion. Where the Allies were remarkably successful was in the exploitation of deception so that right up to the last moment the enemy believed the attack would be across the Pas de Calais. Even as a senior staff officer at HQ Coastal Command he was not privy to the plan and the experience of years of war meant that you did not ask questions. When briefing crews before an operation, for example, the position of U-boats might be given but you never asked where such information had come from – the assumption was that it was obtained from fishing boats or agents along the French coast, there being no inkling it was derived from ULTRA – and the underlying principle was that the less you knew the less you could divulge if you landed in the bag. *Mr Judd*, Station Nav O at an OTU in Bomber Command on D-Day, commented that on the eve all were aware that some major air operation was underway but they had no idea of what exactly was afoot until they heard the early morning news. The secret was very well kept. *Mr Ralph Fellows* said that from about March squadron personnel were aware of the build-up and, as a Dakota navigator, he was involved in numerous glider-towing and releasing exercises but about a week before the landings the station was sealed off with no telephone calls out, no mail in or out, and all confined to the camp. About four days beforehand they were taken to Netheravon to study a huge model of a particular coastline. They were then tasked to paint aircraft and hawsers and by this time it was obvious that something was up, but up to a week before they were not in the picture.

Lord Bramall too remembered the uncertainty. "Up to 2/3 June nobody knew where we were going. We were incarcerated behind barbed wire with armed sentries, and finally given a child's attaché case with maps of Normandy. Till then we had no idea what was going on. It was impossible to tell us. Tremendous activity was taking place around the Solent. By faking wireless nets and activity in Kent, we gave the Germans the impression the real attack was from there. All the ships in Portsmouth could have gone to Dieppe or wherever. Then when I was in the bridgehead the rumours were that we were a diversion and the main attack was somewhere else! So there was tremendous secrecy, but once we were fighting, Monty's view was that the night before a battle we had to be briefed by our company commanders, and we had to brief the soldiers. We explained virtually the whole corps plan. Monty insisted. It was a risk, because somebody might have been captured, but he thought it was worth telling everybody what was planned. Also we knew when things didn't go according to plan!"

Sir Napier Crookenden recalled the extraordinary confidence among the airborne troops. They had trained intensively for a year, they were fit, young and eager, they were well briefed and had good photographic intelligence (fresh photographs came in every day), they knew their objectives. Then they were sealed in a transit camp and cheered when the GOC arrived to announce that the operation was going ahead despite the obstruction of the landing ground by the Germans. They spent the next day awaiting the signal to go; it did not arrive until midday so they were able to buy newspapers announcing the invasion! Their drop was very dispersed but all made their way to the rendezvous; they knew their tasks thanks to the intense, thorough briefing with the use of models. *Sir Napier* stressed that he had no knowledge of the overall strategy. Battalion commanders were not briefed about the location of objectives until their units were sealed in the transit camps, and the security was very tough; indeed after the last pre-invasion exercise the CO of 9th Parachute Battalion was replaced because of a security breach, sent to the Tower of London and court-martialled!

Sir Kenneth Porter, who was Leigh-Mallory's Chief Signals Officer, referred to the tough signals security, to the emphasis on the use of teleprinters, which could not be intercepted, and to the way in which they misled the Germans by constant exercises. Many of his staff knew beforehand where the invasion was going, but not when. D-Day itself was very quiet, just like an exercise; indeed the receiving room operators assumed it was an exercise and the headquarters ship said it was easier than an exercise. The signals organisation had been converted from static to mobile units before the invasion, and the organisation in Normandy would be the same as at home. It had all been practised so many times, and valuable lessons learned from the Dieppe Raid in 1942 had been applied – not least that fighter direction ships were needed in addition to the headquarters ship. Yet there was one great imponderable: the weather. The met. forecast was terrible and although Group Captain Stagg mentioned the possibility of a short break in the bad weather Tedder and Leigh-Mallory wanted to postpone the attack yet again, which would have seriously endangered security.

Many people still wondered: how did we get away with it? As *Lord Craig* put it, "I find it difficult to accept that the Germans could go on believing the main attack would come elsewhere once they witnessed our various landings taking place. And how was security perceived?" *Major Macksey* reminded him how people were conditioned after five years of war to an atmosphere of secrecy; they simply did not talk. *Air Commodore Probert* observed that the German command system must take some of the blame – it was not remotely comparable to that of the Allies. In particular their intelligence organisation was not properly used – often what the intelligence staff said was disbelieved. Their command structure was not integrated and their operational leadership was not prepared to listen. Moreover they were unable to carry out effective air reconnaissance over the mounting area at the critical time. *Dr Boog* referred to the false information being fed to German intelligence: one of the great successes of Allied strategy was making the Germans believe that the landings were going to be further to the north, around Calais – a view reinforced, said *Miss Ward*, by the keeping of a phoney army poised across the Channel from Calais. German agents in Britain were totally taken in by this deception, responded *Dr Boog*: "if you want to deceive an enemy, you have to reinforce his fears. The principal fears were for Calais, and the rocket launching sites near there, and an invasion in this area seemed probable." *Sir Michael Beetham* agreed: deception was a vital factor. Targets throughout France were bombed, so as not to give indications of where the main invasion was going to be. Fortunately, the Allies had by then amassed tremendous resources, so this large scale and widespread bombing was possible.

One particular operation which made life difficult for the Germans was described by *Air Vice-Marshal Furner*, who was serving as squadron navigation officer in 214 Squadron, operating B-17s. "They were fully fitted out with lots of fancy gadgets with names like Mandrel, Pipe Rack, Airborne Cigar and so on, all designed to jam various parts of the spectrum. They were kitted out to carry half a dozen German-speaking operators in the back who listened to RT conversations, identified the frequency and then blasted it. Prior to D-Day we were engaged in flying at least 5,000 ft above the main stream to give them ECM protection. I suppose that was the first time that the letters ECM came into being. Then on 5 June we went to briefing and we thought that this looked a bit different. We were ordered to stooge across the Channel back and forth from about Eastbourne to Dieppe and then in about another 80 miles just south of the Somme, back and forth about eight times. Navigation, they told us, was very important: it had to be accurate. We flew at 27,000 ft and just blasted away on everything we had. What it did was to provide a complete curtain cutting the west of our line from the east of our line. That went on from about 10 pm until 4 am and in the process, I am happy to say, our rear gunner shot down an Me 410. That was my D-Day."

Security was important too in France, as *Group Captain Verity* observed. The Maquis were certainly given general guidelines a long time before D-Day so that they could be properly trained and equipped, and in the detailed operations planning, the resistance forces answering to de Gaulle and others were put together under Eisenhower's headquarters, so as to coordinate with the general planning. However, the French Resistance were not given the finer details of the OVERLORD plan; they did not know where the actual landings were going to be. The only definite information they had was on the evening of the 5th when they were told the landings were going to happen the next day.

The changed roles of the media between then and now, together with the modern difficulties of generating support for military action, were also discussed. *Sir Denis Crowley-Milling* had experienced no problem with the media during the war: there were far fewer of them and they were far less of a menace. They got most of their information from centralised press briefings, and he personally never had to conduct any briefings or interviews with the press, whereas he had been amazed to learn in talking with a Gulf War squadron commander that he had had problems with the media talking to his crews as they climbed out of their aircraft after a sortie.

Lord Bramall, asked about the 10,000 casualties incurred on D-Day – a "staggering" figure by today's standards – pointed out that the casualties on the first day of the Somme were 100,000. "If we had had television the Somme battle couldn't have happened as it did. In OVERLORD it wasn't 10,000 killed; many recovered. For such an enormous operation those were comparatively light casualties; we were invading a hostile country with strong defences. But now that warfare is piped into everybody's home I don't know how you could run a war. You would have to change your ideas very considerably or have some form of censorship. Read the papers of 6 June 1944 and everything is marvellous. If they had actually seen what was happening on OMAHA Beach what would the public attitude have been? Television gives a completely new perspective. OVERLORD was the greatest combined operation the world has ever seen, or is ever likely to see. The Gulf could have been quite nasty, but the bombing was some distance away and the land battle went faster than anybody expected."

The bombing of Caen caused comment: given the lengths the RAF was currently constrained to go to avoid causing casualties it seemed extraordinary to some that the public in World War Two accepted such things as normal. *Charles Messenger* referred to the transportation plan and the number of French civilians it might kill on the very eve of liberation. "The original estimate was something like 80,000 French civilian deaths; then it was slowly whittled down as Bomber Command proved they could do the job fairly accurately; this was a dilemma parallel with the worry about collateral damage. If you were on the ground battlefield and Caen happened to be in the middle of that battlefield then it did not matter – but remember that surprisingly few French civilians were in fact killed during the ground fighting. Most went into their cellars and sat there waiting for the fighting to pass." For *Derek Wood* it was necessary to remember how people felt. "We had all got so used to bombs etc being thrown at us that we had become complacent and expected the same thing was going to happen over there. Moreover all we saw in the papers was 'Caen was heavily bombed in the course of an advance last night etc'. To the average civilian that just meant nothing. He had probably been bombed in his own town or city. You became inured to it; somebody else is getting it; we are very sorry but we are getting on with the war."

Peter Rudd commented from a pilot's point of view: "it was a different world – the war is sometimes described as the end of the age of innocence. When you read today Eisenhower's message sent to every man on D-Day it looks corny. We had been at war five years – I had been through the blitz, with my house bombed. Someone asked me this morning 'what did it feel like?' I didn't feel brave; I was doing a job for which I, like all other aircrew, had volunteered, a job that had to be done. There was a feeling of enormous elation on the day that at last we were back in Europe, having been thrown out four years earlier. It was a different world. Indeed one of my fears was that the war might be over before I got the chance to take part". As *Air Commodore Probert* put it: "It all depends on whether you are involved in a war of national survival."

The Influence of the V-weapons

It was also important to remember that England was itself under attack at the time by the German V1 weapons. *Mr James* mentioned the value of the attacks on Peenemunde and the original V1 launching sites which had much greater launch capacity than the ones that they were eventually forced to use. This was a major pre-D-Day victory without which the V1s pointed at London could have been switched to threaten the D-Day launching area. Indeed, even so, some were launched at the Portsmouth/Southampton area. Had such attacks started a week earlier, coincident with D-Day, or earlier still – which was of course the plan – they could have caused very serious embarrassment. So this was one of the great successes of the war, made possible by dedicated intelligence work on the part of some humble people in Poland and the Baltic countries who fed the stuff back. Nor should the photo recce and interpretation be forgotten, including the role of the girl at Medmenham who spotted the V1 in the Baltic. All these things came together in a most extraordinary story which was a necessary precursor to the success of D-Day.

Mr Nutting, who was an Air Technical Intelligence Officer, added to this from his own experience. "It was important that tangible evidence on V1 and V2 weapons and their launching sites be obtained at the earliest opportunity after a bridgehead had been established. A temporary attachment to the Royal Navy's Technical Intelligence team was arranged for me, in No. 30 Assault Unit, Royal Marine Commandos. As a graduate physicist, trained on entry to the RAF as a signals officer, I was posted to work under ACAS(I) on enemy radio, radar, navigational aids, bomb aiming and infra-red techniques. I had an opportunity to study the radar equipment which was recovered from the Bruneval raid. Before being posted to the Western Desert in the latter part of 1942, my brief was extended to other forms of scientific examination for (the then Dr) R.V. Jones, ADI(Science). In the D-Day period, the aim was to seize technical material; if possible, this was to be done before the enemy had removed or destroyed the evidence, or before the arrival of our own troops who might wreck the equipment. The first target was a V1 launch pad with no visible structure. This was in the Neuilly la Foret area, not far from Isigny-sur-Mer, and at that time about 15 miles beyond the American bridgehead. Before we could dig in for the night, after landing on Utah Beach, a solitary aircraft dropped anti-personnel clusters, causing 30% casualties before we had even started our work. The next morning we passed through the American lines and, armed to the teeth, were able to make a successful survey. The Germans had camouflaged the site with turf, laid over the concrete apron. The German modus operandi was to have many concrete bases ready for use by a number of mobile 'doodle bug' launching units. Each ramp would be permanently oriented, though suitable for several targets such as Southampton, Portsmouth or London. The mobile Wachtel Troop would move in and set up for a day's firing, and then move on to another site a few miles away.

Certainly the countering of the V1s (and later the V2s) caused much diversion of effort. *Mr Cox* said that Leigh-Mallory referred at one point to the Cabinet being very exercised by the attacks and stated that he was worried lest he be forced to divert too much of his effort away from the French railways. *Sir Michael Beetham* agreed that the V weapons caused great concern; while their military value was limited they did cause large resources to be switched to countering them – and ADGB did very well against them once they were organised. *Dr Boog* said Hitler had wanted to use the weapons indiscriminately. *Boog* had talked to the people who designed the V-weapons, now living in America, and they said that they were convinced that the weapons could be made accurate enough to hit precise targets. However, Hitler wanted to use the weapons before they had reached that level of development, and so they never became the precision pieces he wanted. As *Dr Goulter* commented, the fact that they were not precision weapons added to their psychological effect, and *Sir Freddie Sowrey* pointed out the parallel with the Iraqi Scuds in the Gulf War, where much air effort had to be concentrated on the weapon sites.

The Commanders

Several groups discussed the senior commanders and their relationships at length. In one of them *Major General McNeill* considered that differences between leaders had tended to be exaggerated by historians. He discounted, too, the many reports of animosity and jealousy between the Army and RAF for, in his experience, much of that died out in the 1930s. In the Desert War he had seen squadrons operating on an extraordinary light administrative tail and a marked feature was the close cooperation and mutual regard that existed between the two Services – though of course each had its prima donnas. He agreed with *Mr Humphrey Wynn* that the old informality of the DAF which allowed people to get on well together was replaced in Normandy by an enlarged hierarchy, more rank, more red tape, all of which served to exacerbate the personal differences which did occur, whereas an important factor in the desert was that all lived under the same conditions, which boosted the cameraderie. *Group Captain Richardson* said that during his time as C Nav O at HQ Coastal Command he had close dealings with Group Captain John Searby, his opposite number at HQ Bomber Command, who made no secret of the inter-Group strife and rivalry which preceded the formation of the Pathfinder Force. *Air Vice-Marshal Oulton* agreed: in such conflicts it was the vehement leaders who achieved results but inevitably they had differing views as to how to win the day; vehement people approached every problem with different perspectives which reflected their respective personalities. If a leader was to achieve results he had to be allowed to run the show; though relations might be fine at the squadron and infantry brigade level, by the time you got to the heads of Services or of theatres you were bound to have conflicting views. So it was a happy chance when you got a Montgomery and a Coningham in a particular situation where they were fitting hand in glove. In others they wouldn't and then the Eisenhowers would come into play, smoothing the whole thing over as well as they could.

Mr Roland Beamont agreed that the misunderstandings and lack of cooperation occurred more often at the staff level than at unit level. "In Normandy there was never any lack of understanding and cooperation between our forward liaison officers and the army chaps they were helping, and it worked both ways. We had fighter pilots up in the forward positions controlling the cab-ranks and they came back with an enormous respect for the soldiers on the ground and the nasty job that they had to do. In recent years I have had a flow of correspondence, mostly unsolicited, containing interesting insights into this. One of these came recently from a chap who was a platoon commander dug-in on the roundabout on the south side of the Nijmegen bridge in October 1944. He described in great detail sitting in his slit trench keeping out of the way of 88mm fire and watching a finger four, as he described them, of Tempests patrolling overhead, which were obviously from my outfit. He concluded by saying 'thank God for the Air Force in Normandy, we would have been lost without you'. I have had a number of letters from soldiers like that, who I don't know, all saying exactly the same thing; their appreciation on the ground of our support was enormous. I think that at the same level we had an enormous appreciation of what they were doing."

At many of the higher levels too, the cooperation was excellent, as for example *Sir Kenneth Porter* mentioned in relation to inter-service signals liaison, coordinated by the Joint Signals Board. Yet there could be practical difficulties such as that explained by *Air Vice-Marshal Feesey*: "The ground force commander, at what we would now call the operational level, typically wants to move forward to be as close to his troops as he can; it is good for their morale, it is good for his morale and it shortens his lines of communications. The air commander, on the other hand, may want to stay back where his headquarters are, where his communications are and where his troops are. As we heard this morning 'Mary' Coningham stayed back at Uxbridge – he felt he had to – and Monty went forward across the Channel where he felt he had to be. That still seems to be a problem sometimes today."

In another group there was much discussion of individual commanders. *Lord Bramall* spoke about Eisenhower. "He was an extremely nice man. It was important to have at the top someone who everybody trusted. Secondly he was bitten by the Allied bug. He really did want to make sure this was a team effort, not favouring either British or Americans. Although bombarded by pressures from a lot of strong characters he was capable of taking the really big decisions that a Supreme Commander must. He had no real experience of land battlefields, and his control of armies was probably doubtful, but he made extremely big decisions, particularly deciding not to go ahead on 5 June and not to delay the invasion on 6 June. That was his decision and his alone, though he had conflicting advice. Also he persisted with the airborne landings, after the Air C-in-C had been very pessimistic about success, particularly in the American sector. As a Supreme Commander he cut a very good image, very trustworthy."

"He also handled Montgomery very well," *Lord Bramall* continued. "Montgomery was not easy to work with. I don't think I can blame Monty before D-Day: all that publicity helped ensure confidence in the country and elsewhere that the invasion was going to work. I excuse to some extent his white lies about the battle of the eastern sector, mentioned this morning. He did have a very big problem, and had to keep up the confidence of his troops. If he had actually said his attack had not achieved what it was supposed to and had not reached open ground, that would have been giving the Germans a useful trick. He had to make a virtue out of necessity, but he did annoy a lot of people at SHAPE who did not understand. Unfortunately, though he was only doing 75% of everything he wanted to, he could not bring himself to admit 25% failure even privately to people like Coningham, Tedder and Eisenhower. People did not really understand his grand strategy and were not tolerant when he had to modify it a bit. There are extenuating circumstances, but when he went on about a single thrust into Germany he really was tackling Eisenhower head-on. It was quite unnecessary, because even if it had been the right military answer there was no way at that stage that Patton was going to be grounded and give all his supplies to Montgomery or that all the Americans could be told it was nothing to do with them. Again Eisenhower proved he had the overall responsibility. He said, 'sorry, Monty'. Really Monty was disgraceful with his boss over that, and all his staff told him so."

Asked about the qualities of wartime leadership, *Lord Bramall* replied: "You have to dominate, not just have people obeying orders. You must be physically very robust. You must have a clear idea of priorities. That was one of Monty's great strengths: he always knew exactly what he wanted to do, what was important, and what he could leave to the Staff. He had a master plan he was determined to keep to. You also need good administration and logistics, and you must be courageous mentally and physically. Monty was not always in the front line like Marshal Ney or even Rommel, but his Headquarters was always near, and he was never put off by a bit of shelling. With good leadership people will know who's the boss. You must have a clear brain, a very clear idea of what you want to do and must not be put off, so that you can deal with enemy reactions. The Air Force qualities I would have thought would be the same."

Sir Frederick Rosier, concurring, described a typical briefing: "After two minutes Monty began: 'I've brought you all together to tell you that I've made a plan. Now when I say I've made a plan, it's not quite right because I've made a plan in conjunction with the Air Force. The Air Force and I have made a plan. And every plan must have an intention. Now it's my intention to go to Tripoli. Gentlemen, I'm going to Tripoli, and I'd like you to know it's the Air Force's plan, too. We're all going to Tripoli together.' Nobody was in any doubt! What a man!"

Sir Patrick Dunn added: "The quality which Coningham disliked and admired in Field Marshal Montgomery, and shows in Augustus John's portrait, was a slight megalomania. He said, Monty doesn't want to be an Everest in a range of mountains – he wants to be a Kilimanjaro in a plain!"

Flight Lieutenant Diamond, a Bomber Command navigator, was struck by the contrast between some RAF commanders and Montgomery. "Dowding was in his office most of the time. Harris inspired people to go out night after night after night. He was C-in-C Bomber Command from February 1942 and spent two years sending aircraft over Germany, with a very low survival rate. Without them the enemy would have had more hardware, and a strong Luftwaffe. I do not think he ever visited us, but somehow he inspired us." *Lord Bramall* agreed. "Nobody said, that bloody old man, why doesn't he get off his backside! There were three things, stamina, leadership quality and personality which somehow percolated out of his office through the body of the force in the most remarkable way. He clearly had an extremely clear brain for priorities and knew exactly what he wanted to do. If you pick these three things, I think Harris illustrates it in his way and Monty in his. They needed to do things differently."

One other question relating to Montgomery was brought out by *Air Commodore Probert* who wondered if it was right that when Monty was appointed to take command he should be allowed to bring with him his key airmen – Coningham and Broadhurst – with whom he had got used to working in the Mediterranean. *Probert* remembered speaking to Sir William Dickson on this, for he had been AOC 83 Group – he had built it up and had every reason to expect to be commanding it for OVERLORD. To his surprise he was told seven months beforehand that Montgomery wanted Broadhurst to replace him while he went out to Italy. Typical of Dickson he bore no ill-will, no malice, and said "it's one of those things – it was reasonable for Monty to bring the man he knew". But was it really right to play around with the key commanders who were deeply into the preparation for OVERLORD at this relatively late stage? Should not Portal have said "Dickie can do the job, let him get on with it"? However, as *Lord Craig* commented, it would have been very difficult to push that one hard under all the circumstances; the name of the game was to get on and win.

Of the senior RAF commanders only one aroused much debate, perhaps because – as *Sir Michael Beetham* said – the air force command structure worked superbly well, apart from Leigh-Mallory and his relations with others. *Mr Cox* believed that one of Leigh-Mallory's biggest problems stemmed from his rather pompous and reserved manner. His diary, which he dictated to one of his staff officers every evening, revealed his own very high opinion of himself, and the insufferable air of superiority which would grate so much with the distinctly down to earth approach of the Americans. *Mr Jackson*, however, paid him tribute: "I get a little bit fed up with people assassinating Leigh-Mallory all the time. He was an architect of tactical air power, ever since the days when he was Commandant of the Army Cooperation School in the 1920s, and I think that for the success of the invasion and its various tactical air operations we owe him a great debt of gratitude." *Sir Kenneth Porter*, who knew him well, remembered him as kind and generous, not clever but shrewd.

He had been wrong during the Battle of Britain over the Big Wing dispute, but the residual ill-feeling was not responsible for his problems in 1944, and he was a firm believer in army cooperation. Unfortunately Coningham disliked him, and whereas Coningham rightly preferred medium bombers, Leigh-Mallory favoured the heavies. Nevertheless, *Sir Kenneth* said, Leigh-Mallory certainly had the confidence of Portal and was chosen by him after Normandy to take over Air Command South-East Asia.

Aspects of Air Operations

That air superiority was a vital factor in the Operation's success was unchallenged. "Air power was everything to us," said *Major Macksey* who, as a tank man, appreciated the significance of Allied air superiority and witnessed nearly all the unopposed mass attacks on German positions. *Wing Commander Roland Beamont*, who commanded a Tempest wing, described its task as "primarily air superiority – we were thought of, at the time, as potentially the best fighter available for the medium altitude war, below 20,000 ft. We were also good at ground attack with guns at the beginning before bombs were put on. As the D-Day operations developed we were being put more and more into air superiority, because we would clearly outclass the German fighters if any appeared, but we were still being put on quite a lot of ground attack because it was a very accurate weapons platform. Then the V1 interrupted and we were stuck on that for two solid months."

In reply to a question about close support system *Sir Frederick Rosier* commented, "I don't like the words cab-rank. If you just have people sitting up there waiting, you're squandering time. We did NOT use cab-rank but were great believers in armed reconnaissance. A good Army Bomb Line was necessary. When you sent aeroplanes on armed reconnaissances they were always available to be diverted to a target requested urgently by the Army. There was little point in sitting on the ground waiting for Army calls for close support. It was far better to keep them active in the air and bring them down when needed." *Lord Bramall* seized upon this point. "I think bomb line ought to be one of the main things that comes out. A realistic one, to really let the Air Force get on with it," and went on to remark that, "the ideal bomb line was a river or railway, something easily identifiable". *Squadron Leader David Robertson*, referring to Gulf War experience, stated that, "As a navigator on a high-tech Tornado,

Royal Air Force Staff College. Directing staff and advanced staff course 86 to whom the Royal Air Force Historical Society are indebted for hosting the symposium on 'Overlord' and contributing so effectively to its success

Group Captain Ian Madelin in discussion with Air Chief Marshal Sir Frederick Rosier as participants leave for the Brooke-Popham Lecture Theatre

Going to the Brooke-Popham Lecture Theatre after morning coffee

Left to right: Royal Air Force Historical Society Membership Secretary Jack Dunham, Editorial matters Tony Richardson, Treasurer Desmond Goch

Group seminar

Group seminar with Wg Cdr Andy Brookes of the college directing staff in the chair

Another view of group seminar with Wg Cdr Andy Brookes

which could bomb in a bucket, but could miss by a long way, I was absolutely horrified to find bomb lines so near to troops. In the Gulf, for example, there's no way 600 yards was anywhere near sufficient. With the bombing accuracies available in 1944, who set the bomb lines?" *Sir Frederick Rosier* responded that, "You could have bomb lines very much less than that when you used fighter bombers, ones accustomed to doing the job. But Strategic Forces like Bomber Command – No."

Squadron Leader Steve Murkin followed up the point about armed reconnaissance and asked what sort of mechanism there was for troops to call them. *Sir Frederick Rosier* responded, "Actually a very good mechanism, developed in the Desert. I think that was when we began to understand that no single service could win the war, and you all had to help each other. Just before CRUSADER, in November 1941, signals procedures were introduced and we were developing the passing of information from those wanting help to people who could give it. It got better and better and from D-Day onwards and with improved VHF radios it worked extremely well." He added that they would talk directly to the aeroplanes. In elaboration of this point, *Lord Bramall* commented, "You had two things, and you could have something in between. You had the pre-planned and you could have the emergency. Every Brigade had an Air Support Signals Unit that went right back to where requests were considered by a joint control."

"But the Forward Air Controllers came into their own in Normandy. They were able to talk to aircraft, and say how the target was to be marked. But the rest of it was rather like ringing up for a taxi. If there was something on armed reconnaissance in the area, then the aircraft could be tasked to do the job; if not, you worked through a tasking organisation. I don't know how many FACs there were, but they were increasing, and very much in evidence in a particular attack, able to control any aircraft flying in the area. Targets were marked by smoke – usually artillery smoke – or there might be something like a road or a railway they could refer to."

In response to *Squadron Leader David Sharpe* who queried whether the Americans used FACs and could have called in some close air support when they had problems at OMAHA, *Lord Bramall* pointed out that, "they could have used the Command Ships, but the beach defences were within fifty or a hundred yards of the people fighting there. They really would not have been a very good target. The time to do it was before you got in. On the beach you were too close to them, and had to get by on your own. You couldn't get any tanks ashore because they sank in the choppy waters. That was the trouble."

Not surprisingly, the subject of airborne operations raised much comment and *Mr Humphrey Wynn* commented particularly on "the immeasurable courage of the Army glider pilots. When you think of being in control of a Hamilcar which was a big aircraft, once you're released and at night you've no power to do anything but to go down wherever you are and whatever the obstacles. They did this with tremendous courage." *Squadron Leader Chapman* enquired about the types of location aids available to the tug and glider pilots for their precision landings. *Mr Ralph Fellows*, a pilot of 271 Squadron of 46 Group and based at Down Ampney, did two Horsa tugs on 5/6 June, and commented "that REBECCA and EUREKA was supposed to be available but it often wasn't, but we had had the benefit of a good scale model and a PRU film sequence of the run-in for each of the three landing zones at which there was to be an illuminated T. We had communication with the glider pilots as long as the tow rope was connected but once they'd pulled off they were on their own in finding their T." *Air Vice-Marshal Oulton* observed that the system relied on the REBECCA/EUREKA equipment which was a beacon on the ground which was interrogated by the aeroplane and told you where you were and how far away. But if intensive bombing of the area had been carried out the facility was often no longer available, whereas naval ships had Decca which fixed their position almost within a hundred yards; if the towing aircraft had been similarly equipped they would have had no navigation problem and it could easily have been done. *Mr Fellows* reinforced this point from his own experience in delivering back-up equipment for the attack on the Merville Battery. "Three tugs involved in the attack were to take off one hour after us. Our problem was, in coordination with the glider pilot, to release at the correct time. He had Gee radio equipment to get to the rendezvous. Everything went well. There was a new Gee-Chain kept for us and we saw the coast of Normandy approaching just as had been shown in the scale model at Netheravon which we'd pored over. Landmarks were picked out and everything seemed to be going well until Bomber Command went to work on the Battery and everything disappeared – dust and debris came flying up towards us at about 1,000–1,500 ft. Fortunately, this possibility had been anticipated and we had as a landmark a hollowed-out wood which served the desired purpose for the glider pilot who picked out his landing mark at the last moment and muttered briefly, 'Cheerio, see you back in England'." He added that "the operation came close to being a disaster for of the three Horsas that followed, the first's tow rope snapped leaving the glider to land at Odiham, the second one's arrester chute opened above the

Channel and the glider pilot only just managed to make the coast but got about 5 miles from the Battery. The third one got within about 500 yards. They were supposed to meet up with the paratroopers but, instead of the planned 500, only 150 made the RV. Nevertheless, they got into the Battery and by 5 o'clock spiked the guns which commanded the beaches. Had they failed the Navy was standing by to open up on the target at 0530 – our signal was just in time." *Mr Talbot Green* made the further point that "One of the things that wasn't mentioned this morning was that when the glider tug pilots discovered there was triple-A and started taking evasive action, when they released the gliders they weren't sufficiently high for the gliders to actually go the extra distance to the target. They just ran out of air. I don't think that had been allowed for in the planning where they said the tug will take you within x miles of your DZ and release you. That is partially why they got scattered and were not released where the planners assumed they would be released."

The Aircraft Employed

Wing Commander Roland Beamont commented on his pilots' confidence in the Tempest V which was, "briefly, a Typhoon with three years further development getting all the bugs that were in the early Typhoon out and putting some major improvements in, including a thin elliptical wing which made it look a bit like a Spitfire, and a very much uprated performance. It was a fine aeroplane. In our working up with the first two squadrons all the pilots were enjoying it and morale was really up and we could see that as we were based at Dungeness and were about the closest airfield that you could get to France, just at the right time for the opening of this big scene, with the best aeroplane for the job, so we were in a very good position." The diversion from 15 June to defence against the V1 was something of a disappointment.

Following up the point about the Typhoon bugs, *Air Marshal Sir Denis Crowley-Milling* observed that the aircraft had been put into production before it had completed type-testing. "The problems arose on the production aircraft rather than the prototypes, and boiled down to the manufacture of the sleeve-valves for the Sabre engine and the stress on the tailplane. "After that it was a magnificent aircraft, particularly at low level. It was built like a brick outhouse and if you hit a brick wall you went straight through it. One of his pilots had spun in, and the pilot emerged unhurt after losing the wings, tailplane and engine and being left sitting in the framework of the cockpit."

The effectiveness of the Typhoon as a ground attack aircraft was widely commented upon. *Major Macksey* raised the issue about the accuracy of its rockets, citing the classic case of a Panzer armoured concentration near Mortain remaining virtually undamaged after one attack by twelve aircraft. Responding, *Mr Christopher Shores* said: "About twenty-five years ago I wrote a history of 2nd TAF and interviewed quite a lot of Typhoon pilots and read some of the damage-assessment team results following the Panzer counter-attack and the Falaise Gap. Effectively, the Typhoon rocket had a considerable gravity-drop. If you came in low and fairly level to dodge flak you had to get very close to obtain any worthwhile results. If you attacked in a steep dive, then it became a very much more effective and accurate weapon. At Falaise, the armoured vehicles were caught in huge traffic jams, so the rockets were able to do a lot of damage from diving almost vertically on them. In the counter-attack, with the Panzers moving, the Typhoon's other great strength as a cannon-firing aircraft was being a very stable and accurate gun-platform indeed. The assessment teams found the main damage was done to soft-skinned vehicles bringing up supplies for the Panzers, which had to halt because they'd run out of ammunition and fuel and their support had been destroyed, mainly by Typhoons' cannon fire." Many speakers commented in like manner and *Mr Charles Messenger* added the point that, though follow-up Army operations analysis found few tanks were knocked out, huge numbers were abandoned in one piece, a classic illustration of success in turning back a counter-attack.

Mr Humphrey Wynn commented on the great courage of the Typhoon pilots. "We heard about the power of the German tanks with their awesome 88mm guns. We think of the Typhoons as a ground battle-winning weapons, as they were, but they were terribly vulnerable because they had to fly at very low level. Books on Typhoon operations by John Golley and David Ince have shown that if they attacked any of the radar installations on the French coast they went in pairs at very low level and because of the target on a steady course – there was no jinking and some of these descriptions bring out that, suddenly, one of the pair would disappear, evaporate, from a direct hit. The same thing happened when attacking German tanks – when hit by an 88mm that was that. This was the very personal aspect of a great operation." *Wing Commander Roland Beamont* agreed, saying it was "the Typhoon professionals who did the close rank work. That became a highly developed art, both from the point of view of the forward air controllers and the chaps concerned who were flying incredible sorties. They would fly a 15 to 20 minute sortie from an advanced airstrip, go in through all the flak, fire their rockets and drop the bombs, back again and load up, and go on doing it all through the day with very high casualties." *Group Captain Dacre* asked "Was it solely the cab-rank system which ensured air support arrived at the right moment, and what sort of ground-air communications were there to ensure that there were not friendly-fire errors in the melee of battle?" *Sir Dennis Crowley-Milling* responded "It was certainly of great importance to have the aircraft in the right place at the right time. There was always cab-rank more or less permanently airborne, which could be called down by the FAC on targets of opportunity, using clock codes or smoke to indicate the target. Controllers in Austers also occasionally marked targets with smoke. There might only be four aircraft in the cab-rank at any one time, but that was usually enough." He went on to stress that the Typhoons were given a delineated area for the patrols before take-off, and therefore had some idea of where the enemy and their troops were.

The use of one of the key elements of air power, the heavy bomber, generated much discussion. *Major Macksey's* view was that, "When the techniques were right, it was correct; in an attack such as that on Caen where the bombing made rubble and craters, it was wrong; in any case it was ridiculous to bomb in the evening and not next morning just before the land attack went in. The Germans were thus given ample time to recover. GOODWOOD was another matter; the bombing went well – the most effective attacks being by the medium bomber using ground-burst weapons. Le Havre was a superb example, which I saw myself. Splinter bombs were used right across the front, with crater bombs further in. We were able to drive right through, using flails in the minefields, and got through fairly easily – the bombs absolutely stunned the Germans and we met little resistance for up to 2,000 yards. The next night, however, I was ordered into a cratered area to attack an area which was still holding out – this was impossible, and I had to pull out. Overall I thought the heavy bomber attacks were extremely effective and gave us enormous confidence." *Mr Sebastian Cox* pointed out: "It was the original raids on the marshalling yards which had first sown the seed in Leigh-Mallory's mind over using the heavy bombers in direct support of the army. He became extremely concerned in the period immediately after D-Day when the Army was becoming bogged down in the bocage that the Germans would be able to bring in sufficient troops to contain the Allies and isolate the bridgehead leading to a bloody stalemate. The AOC-in-C therefore seized on the evidence that Bomber Command could hit a 1,000 yd box accurately, and started to consider ways to deploy this power to boost the ground forces out of the bocage and into the open country beyond. Interestingly, in view of the controversy it caused, Leigh-Mallory had been aware of the cratering problem, and had said that the RAF must avoid creating too many craters, though he never explained quite how! The subsequent bombing of Caen remained a mystery to historians. The 'bomber box' was in all probability moved because of the fears raised about friendly casualties, but it had ended up in a position where it missed both German forward and support positions and merely killed a lot of Frenchmen and devastated the city." He thought it "most likely that this was the result of it passing through too many sets of ground and air headquarters, and thus causing confusion and attenuation of the purpose of the strikes and allowing fear of friendly casualties to move it from the intended German targets. But the actual reason might never be known with certainty." *Sir Denis Crowley-Milling* commented "AM Coningham said it would have been far better if he had put his Typhoons into the Caen area, and kept the heavies well away from the city." *Brigadier Watkins* concurred – in his view "It had done nothing but create a physical obstacle which Allied tanks could not cross. I think the misuse of the strategic bombers was one of the great lessons of the campaign. Much of the blame rested with Army Commanders, who became reluctant to commit themselves without massive air support, often the wrong type. This was perhaps understandable, since it is not generally realised that the intensity of the infantry fighting in Normandy rivalled that of the Somme." Picking up this point, *Mr Cox* commented: "However, many of the attacks by the strategic bombers were successful. The bombing of Villers Bocage soon after D-Day, for example, had successfully disrupted a German counter-attack." This view was reinforced by *General Crookenden* who considered that Harris had not appreciated how accurate his bombers had become. "We on the ground were delighted. The bombers created a great mess at Caen – but they were always welcome." The inevitability of mishaps had to be accepted, of course, and he emphasised that "Soldiers accepted 'blue-on-blues', which were very common during the campaign from both artillery and air power. I was personally attacked several times, but they were such battle-winning assets that we accepted them."

Blue-on-Blue Incidents

Several groups discussed the problem of blue-on-blue accidents which sometimes stemmed from a breakdown in coordination. *Wing*

Commander Roland Beamont referred to "a classic case two weeks after D-Day when Normandy-based Typhoons, Johnny Baldwin's wing, were sent off one morning, not to go and attack the bomb-line, but to go up Channel, to look for maritime targets, and there was a force of reported enemy ships coming down the Channel and he had two squadrons of rocket-armed Typhoons and when they found this lot – there was a cruiser and couple of escorts – they attacked them and that was total lack of coordination between the Navy and Fighter Command, and even between two naval sectors. I don't know what the actual terminology is, but at that time there was a naval force responsible for North of the Thames and another one for the Channel and this lot North of the Thames sent this force down the Channel without telling the Channel lot that they were coming. There were lots of casualties." *Mr Cox* added that this had been a problem for the air forces. Leigh-Mallory had refused to fly one paratroop mission requested by the Army after D-Day because the lift would have been required to fly over the invasion shipping. Leigh-Mallory's diary records his HQ receiving a complaint from Admiral Vian that too many Allied aircraft were flying over his ships! The C-in-C of the Allied Expeditionary Air Force had recorded that he was not sure if he was supposed to take the complaint seriously – but he did not intend to do so!"

In land operations it was the delineation of the bomb line which presented the greatest difficulty. *Sir Freddy Sowrey* recalled that in the Desert War "it was quite often the air force's reconnaissance which told the Army where their front-line troops were, so helping the Army to establish a realistic bomb line – safe for their own troops – yet effective because one doesn't want to be attacking the enemy's rear echelons, one wants to attack their forward echelons because those are the sticking points." As was pointed out by *General Crookenden*, however, "a 6,000 yard bomb line was used at Caen for the first time, to be on the safe side". *Sir Denis Crowley-Milling* pointed out that "this was really the first campaign in which the strategic bomber had been used in a tactical role, and most of the problems stemmed from that. Lack of experience and familiarity meant that, for example, the ground troops used orange squares to delineate the forward positions, but some B-17s had mistaken these for markers and bombed them." *Sir Frederick Rosier* cited another occasion when, "A Canadian Group had dropped some markers in the wrong place and the later bombers attacked there. The colour of the day was the same as the markers so that the more our troops tried to show they were friendly, the more bombs were dropped." Desperate phone calls to Bomber Command were futile for the HQ said "We're very sorry we can't – they're on their bombing frequency."

Brigadier Watkins wanted to put the record straight and pointed out that whilst there was a tremendous amount of blue-on-blue in Normandy, it was by no means all the result of air attacks. He reflected that "the Gunners are not known in the Army as 'The Drop Shorts' for nothing. In close country such as the bocage with aircraft travelling at several hundred knots it was inevitable. Although there would be a lot of cursing and swearing, and much deployment of yellow smoke by forward troops as soon as a Typhoon appeared, it was nevertheless recognised as one of the realities of war." *Mr Cassel* recalled a raid on the night of 7 August on German concentrations which had been marked by 8 Group and were successfully attacked by Bomber Command. *Major Macksey* had witnessed this particular operation when, incidentally, the ground forces had been pulled back 2,500 yards, and commented how superbly executed it had been. *Air Commodore Probert* later recalled that the targets "were initially marked by artillery star shells to help the markers. The bombers were also instructed not to bomb unless they were sure the markers had been correctly identified because of the close proximity of friendly troops, which indicates that some lessons were learned from the earlier disasters."

Air Space Control

Recalling Gulf War experience and the crucial importance of air space control, *Squadron Leader Whittingham* of the Advanced Staff Course queried how the Allies controlled 11,500 aircraft and continued: "Arguably, navigation systems, radar and aircraft kit weren't as good as today's so how did you separate aircraft – by established procedures, by height?" Responding, *Group Captain Richardson* commented "Such arrangements weren't possible with different aircraft with different performances, coming from different places, and there was no overall controller as there would be today. It was accepted that some collisions were inevitable." *Air Vice-Marshal Oulton* added that "Another factor was the chance of bombs hitting aircraft at lower altitudes" but he pointed out that "Even in the 1,000-bomber raids the operational analysis assessment was that only one collision would occur and this proved to be accurate." *Sir Frederick Rosier* recalled that certain defined routes were used for aircraft covering the invasion area and *Mr Sidney Goldberg* mentioned the three fighter direction tenders, Nos 13, 216 and 217 with combined naval and RAF crews which carried radar and Y service equipment and played some part in coordinating the flow of aircraft across the Channel. But, as *Wing Commander Roland Beamont* pointed out, procedural methods such as sanctuary levels which are a feature of today's air defence tactics were certainly not employed in those days. He added that "the planning and coordination of the operations was superb and my impression at that time was one of complete confidence in what went on in Headquarters which had tremendously experienced staffs".

Flak

The effects of ground fire on attacking aircraft generated much discussion and it was *John Herrington's* view that we have repeatedly under-estimated its significance. The German box barrage which they developed in front of targets against the bomber stream in the Second World War presented a formidable defensive screen – they mounted numerous light ack-ack guns on one side of the runway and the same on the other side and then coned them over the centre as soon as the attacking aircraft were heard. "There was no way that you could not go through the cone," and as *Wing Commander Roland Beamont* reflected, "that is exactly what happened in some of the airfields in Iraq." As to the battle for Normandy, the Typhoons went into the flak on every sortie, every target was flak defended – "it wasn't weight of fire that was so effective but close to it was the rate and density of fire that was going to get you". *Squadron Leader Gordon Buckley* agreed that his Iraq experience was similar. "What you actually saw yourself was this whole barrage of flak going up – and it was just a whole lead wall. That was the thought that was going through your mind."

The Maritime Aspect

Three particular aspects of the D-Day maritime operation figured in the discussions: inter-service cooperation, improvisation, and the operations of Coastal Command. *Wing Commander Evans* commented that while the seminar had focused, quite rightly, on the application of air power during OVERLORD, to start with it was essentially an amphibious operation. *Air Commodore Stockwell* reflected on his own experience. "Certainly with the Royal Navy, serving in Coastal

Command, I think we can say we worked hand in glove, we had the convoys to protect and they used us for that protection." He thought that cooperation was first class in the ranks of the aircrews who flew and in the crews of the ships, and in the Commands at the Headquarters. Neither wanted to see the waste of the very slender assets available for reconnaissance in the oceans, protection of the convoys and sinking of the U-boats.

The effect of the anti-U-boat operations was raised by *Air Vice-Marshal Oulton*, who said that Operation CORK had been significant in keeping the U-boats out of the Channel. The anti-U-boat campaign of 1943 achieved the objective, albeit temporarily, of forcing them on the defensive. Had we not been able to stop the depredations of the U-boats, the OVERLORD operation would not have been possible in 1944. Had it been delayed for one year, the tremendous German advances in U-boat design (Type 21) and propulsion methods would have enabled them to resume the Atlantic Battle, leaving us little chance of mounting the Second Front – a close-run thing. We managed firstly to pin the U-boats down just at the right time and long enough to allow supplies and personnel to pour across the Atlantic. Secondly, the CORK operation closed the Channel two days before, and for about fourteen days after, the start of the landings in Normandy, so permitting the mass of shipping free access to the beaches – a vitally important aspect of the operation.

Group Captain Richardson, C Nav O, HQ Coastal Command, endorsed the comments on the touch and go nature of the Atlantic Battle, mentioning the heavy losses up to spring 1943, a period when we were unable to obtain information because of changes in the Enigma system and our cryptographers were blind. However, once we managed to close the reconnaissance gap, in which the Azores base played a vital part, we were able to pin the U-boats down and so protect the supply route across the Atlantic. *Richardson* also wished to record that Operation CORK was planned to start three weeks before D-Day and carry on indefinitely because 100 U-boats were known to have concentrated in the French Biscay ports and were waiting to slip around the Cherbourg Peninsula to get into the Channel where they would have wrecked the armada. There were another 70 U-boats in the Norwegian/Baltic areas to be used as back-up but Admiral Doenitz instructed them to join the main force in Brest. Our sixty squadrons were committed to preventing any enemy movement into the Channel and the whole area had to be swept by ASV every half-hour throughout the whole period. This huge undertaking posed immense problems with such a variety of aircraft with different performances –

Sunderlands, Catalinas, Wellingtons and Halifaxes were the most important. The plan devised was to operate in a series of boxes so that flexible use could be made of our resources and the whole plan was facilitated by the introduction in 1943 of a new Gee-Chain in south-west England. Before then, aircraft reconnoitred the Bay of Biscay without any means of fixing their position; inevitably, there had been times when they were very wide of the mark and to organise a series of patrols with a feed in every half-hour would have been impossible without it. This relentless programme continued day and night up to D-Day – and the staff had no clue as to when that would be – but its success could be measured by the fact that not a single U-boat passed through the screen though dozens were sunk in the attempt – sixty-seven in the first three days alone. The outstanding success of the CORK operation was very largely due to the Gee navigation aid made available to Coastal Command.

Dr Goulter stated that the preparations for D-Day placed very large strains on the RAF's structure. There was a need to support the land operations, especially in the critical establishment period, but the question was: where were the support resources going to come from? The Air Staff looked primarily towards Coastal Command to supply the aircraft. Originally, the plan was to suspend anti-shipping operations, thus freeing nine squadrons, and something approaching half of the anti-submarine effort was to be channelled into D-Day support work. The Admiralty responded sharply to the suggestion, emphasising quite correctly that while the U-boat threat had been contained, the war against them had not been totally won. The appearance of Schnorkel-equipped U-boats was later seen as a vindication of the Admiralty's concern. It was easy, with hindsight, to suggest that perhaps Portal and other senior staff over-reacted to the call for air support for D-Day, but he had thought there was a danger of too great a shift in resources occurring, and thus exposing vulnerable flanks elsewhere (such as a resurgent U-boat menace). In the end, the large-scale reallocation of Coastal Command's aircraft did not occur.

Responding to a suggestion that the Air Staff had a 'blind spot' with regard to Coastal Command throughout the war, *Dr Goulter* replied that she would not go as far as to suggest, like some writers on the subject, that large-scale resources should have been transferred from Bomber Command to Coastal, especially in the war against the U-boat. The bomber offensive was a vital factor in Allied success. However, the predominance of strategic bombing theory throughout the RAF's pre-war history meant that other ideas on the employment of air power were marginalised, to a greater or lesser extent, and this was certainly the case as far as maritime aviation was concerned. *Sir Michael Beetham* thought that was a very good point. It highlighted the difficulties faced by a CAS, who had to satisfy all the various requests for resources. Portal had to contend with demands coming from Harris, Douglas and his predecessors at Coastal, as well as the Americans calling for assistance at various times. *Dr Goulter* commented that it was a very delicate balancing act; the Allies did very well, and they won the war!

Captain Bruce-Jones, a present day Royal Marine Commando, was amazed at the ability of people to adapt and improvise on the amphibious assets that they had and that the operation was as successful as it was. He wondered if anyone had experience of that adaptation of non-specialised kit. The landing craft in particular were literally jury-rigged for all sorts of different roles during the landing phase – something that we could possibly get away with now with some of our larger landing craft, but certainly not with the smaller ones, which were not sturdy enough. He wondered how much air assets were adapted for special purposes for the D-Day operations. *Mr Sidney Goldberg* thought things were very primitive. "We had most of the P & O fleet laying off Normandy. On the davits which normally held the lifeboats they had landing craft. There was a variety of smaller landing craft slung from the davits. They were lowered into the water and the troops had to climb into them carrying all of their kit and unit stores, clambering down rope ladders and of course some of them fell into the water. It was suited to the circumstances of the time, but it was primitive. The other, larger craft like the LST were themselves seaworthy and came across. Of course the small craft just went up and down in the water; all the people aboard were hopelessly seasick, then had to come off and fight. There was no other choice, no other option, it was that or nothing, you couldn't argue about it, you had no choice in the matter."

Squadron Leader *Colin Miller* added that his Falklands experience could relate to that to some extent. He sailed down on the *Norland*, which was just a North Sea ferry. "On the first morning that we arrived in San Carlos Water we did feel extremely vulnerable, especially on a North Sea ferry with the jets attacking us at regular intervals. When dawn arrived and the Paras which were on *Norland* were put ashore the LPDs from *Fearless* came in to collect them and they off-loaded through a side door, halfway down the deck of *Norland*, in the swell. Because there was no compatibility between landing craft and the ships, a number of Paras with extremely heavy burdens were certainly damaged long before they got to the shore.

Even in the Falklands many years after it was certainly a jury-rigged affair".

Logistics

Charles Messenger commented that logistics were very important and one of the big driving themes: no matter how efficient the ground or air might be they would not reach their goal without logistics. *Squadron Leader Markey* referred to the unopposed beach landing in Saudi Arabia (Gulf War) when millions of tons of stores were shipped ashore. It was absolute chaos, losing equipment for weeks, yet it was nowhere near the scale of OVERLORD. *Lord Bramall* thought the logistic planning for OVERLORD was extremely good. "I would not say there weren't cock-ups – there always are – but we had what we needed: people went in with a certain number of days' rations and we had the unique Mulberry Harbour which meant we could bring stuff over the beaches or use the pontoons. They also quickly ran a PLUTO pipeline so fuel went straight to a Petrol Point. The Gulf War was laid on at pretty short notice, but we had been planning OVERLORD on and off for two years, and the logistic planning was remarkable." *Sir Frederick Rosier* added that from his recollection, one of the great problems there was congestion on the narrow roads. *Lord Bramall* agreed: "they were just like Cornish lanes. About the 19th to 22nd there was a terrible storm and you couldn't actually get across on to the beaches at all. So the whole thing was disrupted, but by natural causes." He thought the logistic planners deserved great credit.

Group Captain Richardson also raised the question of the logistic problem: "If you moved a squadron from the UK to France to one of the newly created strips, you could not just fly in the aircraft; you had to fly in your guidance systems, fuel, weapons, ground crews, which even under good conditions meant moving some 350 men for a squadron of about 15 aircraft." He also suggested a few thoughts for discussion – the courage of the glider pilots, the cost of Typhoon operations and the logistics problems of deploying squadrons to the Continent and making them operational. *Air Vice-Marshal Oulton* observed that the Army's concept of a fighting division was 15,000 infantry and 10,000 supporters – less than one to one; in the Air Force the proportion was nearer fifty to one plus all the associated equipment including fuel which went out at something like two tons a minute. *Dr Goulter* mentioned that when the final plans were being drawn up for the land invasion, the Army was looking enviously towards the RAF's manpower surpluses, and there were suggestions that thousands of RAF recruits be transferred to the Army.

Mr Goch also referred to the supply problem; he thought it was Eisenhower who said that the greatest war-winning weapon was the Dakota. Equally on the American side at the time, they had a petroleum supply problem and they ran their redball highway through parts of Germany to keep up the supplies to the forward columns. The road supply of petroleum and so on was a very important aspect of operations. An unidentified contributor stated that he was in the oil business in 1935 and learnt quite a bit about the German oil industry and the Ploesti field. During the war he had wondered when they would run out of petrol. It was only after the war that one learnt about the Fischer-Trott process, which the South Africans used to produce some very fine high octane fuel. The only refinery in England that the Germans didn't hit was at Shell Haven. All the high octane fuel was coming across the Atlantic and our air forces would have been grounded as far as Merlins and up were concerned if it hadn't been for that fuel coming across the Atlantic.

Charles Messenger said that while air transport and supply were used to maintain the advance there was a dilemma. The Allied airborne army was sitting in England and between D-Day and Arnhem in September, no less than seventeen airborne operation plans were made up. That airborne army consisted of something like four and a half airborne divisions and many of these plans were going to involve at least two of those divisions. MARKET GARDEN involved three, and that was going to tie up a lot of the transport aircraft. He considered this was why air resupply of the ground advance was not used as much as it might have been: there simply were not enough transport aircraft to meet both demands. "The problem is that your resources cake is only finite, and when you come to campaign planning it is a question of trying to weigh up the priorities of how you are going to divide that cake up."

Arising from *Dr Boog*'s observations about lack of training affecting the performance of the German pilots, questions were raised about the Allied system of training. *Mr Wynn* referred to it as virtually the miracle of the operation; the flying training achievement was quite astounding, though at the expense of serious losses in training, particularly at the OTU stage. There were so many built-in risks of weather, unserviceability and aircrew inexperience when crews were working together as a team for the first time. *Sir Michael Beetham*, having mentioned that the RAF was very short of pilots at the time of the Battle of Britain, referred to the impact of the Empire Air Training

Scheme. By 1944 there were huge resources, and the training machine was actually becoming clogged. People who had been trained by the EATS found themselves waiting in Britain for long periods, waiting to get on a squadron.

Responding to a question about the problems of operating from improvised airfields across the Channel *Mr Goldberg* mentioned that the servicing commandos went in on D+1, together with Royal Engineers airfield construction companies, who laid the track and provided facilities for rearming and refuelling. 83 Group actually landed in France from D+1 with the servicing commandos, but the aircraft returned to the UK every evening for about a week; it was only afterwards that 83 Group moved over with their pilots and for a time the pilots had to live in foxholes close to the aircraft. They were not very happy about having their aircraft serviced by strange crews, and this was a serious bone of contention, but ultimately it sorted itself out.

Intelligence and the Luftwaffe

Lord Bramall replied to a question on ULTRA by stressing that, as a humble lieutenant it had passed him by, but that it was undoubtedly of crucial importance in allowing the deployment of the maximum weight of air power to defeat the Mortain counter-attack. He also pointed to its importance in allowing the Allies to set up and gauge the success of the deception operation. His verdict was: "We would not have done nearly as well so soon without it." In similar vein *Charles Messenger* stressed that ULTRA gave the Allied Commanders an excellent insight into the way the Germans were thinking, and "what they were swallowing and what they weren't. If they weren't swallowing it, it could then be amended so they did swallow it." *Martin Kern* stated that ULTRA was used to win the war, not necessarily the battles, although the information was often available within 48 hours, this was of more strategic than tactical use.

Squadron Leader Mark Wordley asked about battle damage assessment. *Sir Frederick Rosier* replied that the Tactical Air Force had a recce wing of three squadrons which undertook both high and low level reconnaissance which was very good indeed. *Sir Freddie Sowrey* stated that the Allies had the ability to reconnoitre from Calais down to Bordeaux if necessary. In contrast several groups and speakers stressed the almost total absence of photographic reconnaissance on the German side. *Sir Freddie Sowrey* thought this showed not only their inability but their lack of strategic foresight. *Cecil James* disagreed, saying that it was not so much lack of strategic foresight, as the sheer lack of resources. The Russian campaign and the air defence of the Reich had absorbed so much of their effort that "they were so stretched they couldn't really do very much", despite the fact that up until 1943 they had been able to photograph 75% of the UK. *Derek Wood* highlighted the inadequate aircraft available to the Luftwaffe, which had very few long-range reconnaissance aircraft in its inventory, and those which it did have were the same type they had been using in 1940. *Desmond Goch* pointed out that the Luftwaffe's failings did not just apply to reconnaissance, but also to pre-emptive action against the crowded airfields and assembly areas in southern England. *Robert Jackson* and *Dennis Harper* both pointed to German efforts to use jets to overcome their lack of recce capability, and *Jackson* and *Derek Wood* both gave credit to the very efficient Air Defence of Great Britain for preventing almost all Luftwaffe attempts to reconnoitre, except for one or two jet sorties in late July or early August, by which time it was too late.

Other faults in the Luftwaffe's intelligence effort were also identified, in particular the lack of weight and poor personnel accorded to the intelligence organisation. *Derek Wood* pointed out that the head of Luftwaffe intelligence was a Lieutenant Colonel, and that the RAF's analysis of him was far from complimentary. He had consistently misled the Luftwaffe during the Battle of Britain, and was known "for his conviviality and his ability to booze and also to tell Goering exactly what he wanted to hear." These were not the qualities required of a good intelligence officer.

Robert Jackson took up this point and said that it extended to other areas of the Luftwaffe. He believed there were more square pegs in round holes in the Luftwaffe than in comparable air forces. In particular, because the Luftwaffe had been proscribed in the inter-war period there were many senior officers who were basically army officers and who were unable to fly and had never had anything to do with aircraft. "So their whole attitude to the business was wrong in the build-up to the operation we are talking about."

Sir Freddie Sowrey was puzzled by the Germans' denigration of their civilian experts. "Why did they not use academics like Solly Zuckerman, who after all was the architect of the Transportation Plan?" Was it merely a national characteristic, or was it the result of Hitler's influence? *Robert Jackson* believed that many of Germany's best scientists and technicians had been Jewish, and had fled. *Derek*

Wood said that there was a rigid classification of people as either military or scientists. The Germans had nothing like a Sunday Soviet, and demarcation was strictly enforced so that even Martini's signals organisation was only concerned with its own narrow area.

10. Chairman's Closing Remarks

During this study day we have not been trying to rewrite history nor even to look for insights that have somehow eluded the numerous and detailed studies of the campaign in Normandy that have been made over the past fifty years. What we have tried to do is to look at some of the key lessons of Normandy, and in particular lessons for airmen, but in a joint-service context. If my talk during the next ten minutes has a theme, then it is the theme of jointery. And if I have a message for the members of the Bracknell Course, who not only make up such an important part of today's audience but are also the only people here who will be able to apply the lessons from today to events in the more distant future, then my message is about the vital need to carry jointery forward in our three Services.

It is difficult to conceive of an operation on the scale of the Normandy invasion ever being launched again. But I suggest that it is not quite so difficult to imagine circumstances that might make necessary an operation of this type, that is to say an operation involving the closest possible interaction between not only the three fighting Services, but perhaps also the support of a nation in arms.

As we heard from today's presentation, the planners for the Normandy invasion faced three main problems. The first of these was to achieve tactical surprise in the face of strategic certainty. The second was to seize and consolidate a bridgehead in the teeth of what would clearly be increasing German resistance. The third was how to build up strength ashore at a faster rate than the German defenders could bring up reinforcements.

All three problems could be cracked only by a joint-service approach. For example, the degree of tactical surprise needed depended on many things, but one of the many important contributions made to this end was made by the Allied air forces, which had enough resources to be able to spread their air activity before the landings so widely up and down the coast of France that no clue was given as to the chosen area for the assault. For each operational sortie flown over

Normandy in the run-up to D-Day, more than two were flown over areas other than Normandy; thus sorties flown against, say, the Pas de Calais during April were indirectly contributing to the success of a landing 150 miles away and two months later. Or take the second problem, the landing of the initial wave of the invasion itself. Probably the most difficult of all the operations of war is an opposed amphibious landing. Yet with massive naval gunfire support at sea, and air supremacy overhead, the Allies pulled it off. Or look at the third problem, the build-up phase. For the Allies, every single man, every piece of equipment and every ton of supplies had to be embarked in southern England, sailed at least 120 miles and then off-loaded, and that through an artificial harbour towed across the English Channel and anchored off the French coast.

In contrast, on the German side, there were six garrison divisions stationed along the coast of Normandy alone, four very good Panzer divisions within about 100 miles of the beaches, and there had been plenty of time to deploy war stocks into the forward areas. The answer to that imbalance, of course, was the massive sea-lift on the part of the Allied navies, and a carefully planned interdiction campaign by the Allied air forces.

Not that this degree of inter-Service cooperation at the highest level was always easily achieved. It was true that by 1944 we had come a long way from the years before the First World War, a situation now eighty years behind us today, but still I suggest worth a small digression. As late as 1910, four years before the outbreak of war that was widely predicted, the British Army had worked out plans with the French for the reception and deployment on the Continent of a British Expeditionary Force. The Royal Navy meanwhile, keen on a purely maritime strategy, had developed sketchy plans for amphibious landings on the German North Sea and Baltic coasts, and was actually refusing to take part in staff discussions on how the British Expeditionary Force was to be moved across the Channel in the first place.

I said that things were much better in 1944, but all was still not sweetness and light. We need only examine the directives governing the use of Allied strategic air power in Europe to be given a glimpse of the divergent views that existed at the highest levels of command. In fact there were three quite different versions of just what the aims of that air campaign were to be.

You will recall the Casablanca Directive for the Combined Bombing Offensive, which read in part "to bring about the progressive destruction of the German military, industrial and economic system and the undermining of the morale of the German people to a point where their capacity for armed resistance is fatally weakened". Bomber Command put its emphasis on the phrase "undermining the morale of the German people", and went perforce for area targets by night. The US Eighth and Ninth Air Forces on the other hand concentrated on the part of the directive that mentioned "the destruction of the German military, industrial and economic system", and they attacked point targets by day. The American and British air commanders were thus each fighting a classic strategic bombing campaign, though in two different ways. But a third and entirely different interpretation of the Casablanca Directive came about when a most important new sentence was added before the directive was finally promulgated. The new sentence read: "This is to be construed as meaning so weakened as to permit the initiation of final combined operations on the Continent." So we had the senior soldiers, sailors and to some extent the political leaders of both countries regarding the strategic bombing campaign as simply a preparation for the invasion of Europe. It was a remarkable lack of common aim, and one that was not resolved until only two months before the Normandy landings when Eisenhower was given operational control of all the Allied air forces in the theatre.

One of the most striking things to come out of today's talks and discussions, I suggest, is the contrast between on the one hand that kind of disagreement or differing perception at the highest levels of command at the time of the Normandy invasion (and there were others); and on the other hand the very close cooperation that existed at the sharp end of all three Services. This is probably a good time to mention three of the other main points that emerged in the eight discussion groups:

a. The essential role of intelligence, including the successful deception of German intelligence (this seems to be a very fruitful area of interest for a future seminar).

b. The overriding importance of jointery at all levels. Lessons were carried forward from North Africa and Italy. It is important not to lose sight of all that today – we have sometimes tended to do it.

c. The vital nature of air supremacy. This was so much part of OVERLORD's success that there is a danger of taking it for granted when we look back. In fact, the air supremacy held by the Allies was the result of a very long and costly struggle over the previous three years or more.

One of the most intriguing questions about this vast enterprise is this. Was its successful outcome inevitable? The answer must be that success was no means assured. The portents were not after all particularly encouraging. Everyone remembered Gallipoli in 1915, where a very costly foothold had been gained from which it then proved impossible to break out. More recently, and only four years before Normandy, there had been the ill-fated expedition to Narvik, a fumbling and ad hoc affair launched without proper resources. Then there had been Dieppe, with all its tragic losses. Only the year before Normandy, the landings in Sicily had been accompanied by badly targeted parachute drops which had scattered our paratroopers over a wide area, and by mis-identifications that caused Allied ships to shoot down a considerable number of our own aircraft. And finally there had been the assault across the beaches at Anzio, which the German defenders had been able to quickly seal off.

It could indeed have gone wrong. What if Hitler had been awakened at once by his hesitant staff once they had received the alert? What if Hitler himself had not hesitated to release the panzer divisions? What if the weather had not held for those first few vital days (and remember that weather forecasting is scarcely perfect today, never mind fifty years ago)? And what if the set-back at OMAHA beach had been repeated at all the other assault beaches? General Omar Bradley was watching events from off-shore on board his command ship, and two and a half hours after the first troops of the US 29th Division went ashore, things were apparently going so badly that Bradley started preparations to re-embark his troops.

Those questions and many others like them will continue for very many years to fascinate students of military affairs. Today we have been able only to skim the surface of one or two aspects of this vast enterprise, but we have had the privilege and great pleasure of hearing from some of the participants who have not only been able to give us their impressions of the events we have been discussing but also – because they are all military historians of note – to put in perspective the events they discussed with us.

Brief though our seminar has been, I very much hope that it has given food for thought to all of us here and particularly to the students of the Advanced Staff Course – the officers who can particularly benefit in a professional sense from the kind of occasion that the RAF Historical Society has arranged here at Bracknell today.

Biographical Notes on the Main Speakers

Air Chief Marshal Sir Michael Armitage KCB CBE

Air Chief Marshal Mike Armitage joined the RAF in 1947. After service with No 28 Fighter Squadron in Hong Kong, he returned to the UK for 3 tours in Flying Training Command before attending the RAF Staff College in 1965. After a tour as PSO to CinC RAF Germany he commanded No 17 Reconnaissance Squadron at Wildenrath, flying Canberra PR7s. Following the ISSC Course in 1970, he then joined the staff of that establishment before commanding RAF Luqa, in Malta, from 1972 to 1974.

After completing the 1975 RCDS Course, he served for two years as Director of Forward Policy in MOD(Air) before going to RAF Germany as Deputy Commander. Further appointments included Directing Staff at the RCDS and Director of Service Intelligence before becoming the first Chief of Defence Intelligence in 1983; in the same year he was appointed KCB. He then became Air Member for Supply and Organization before completing his final tour in the Royal Air Force as Commandant of the RCDS. He retired in 1990.

Sir Michael is a member of the RUSI and IISS. He contributes to professional journals, and is co-author of the book *Air Power in the Nuclear Age* published by MacMillan and by the University of Illinois in 1984 and again in 1985.

Mr John Terraine FRHistS

John Terraine was born in London in 1921 and educated at Stamford School and Keeble College, Oxford. He joined the BBC in 1944 as a Recorded Programmes Assistant and did a variety of work including production of Radio Newsreel, programme assistant in the East European Service, and programme organizer of the Pacific and South African service. In 1963 he became associate producer and scriptwriter of the BBC Television series 'The Great War', for which he received the Screenwriters' Guild Documentary Award. He left the BBC in 1964 and scripted 'The Life and Times of Lord Mountbatten' for Thames Television in 1966. In 1974 he was scriptwriter and narrator of the BBC series 'The Mighty Continent'.

He is the author of many books including ten titles about the First World War, and is also the founding President of the Western Front Association. His other books include a biography of Lord Mountbatten, *The Mighty Continent* and *Business in Great Waters* which is a study of the U-boat campaigns in both World Wars. In 1985 he wrote *The Right of the Line*, a major study of the RAF's part in the Second World War and now a standard text on the subject.

In 1982, to mark his contribution to military history, John Terraine received the Chesney Gold Medal, the highest award of the Royal United Services Institute for Defence Studies. In 1987 he became a Fellow of the Royal Historical Society.

Field Marshal the Lord Bramall KG GCB OBE MC JP

Field Marshal Bramall, then a Lieutenant in the King's Royal Rifle Corps, landed in Normandy on Juno Beach on D + 1 and was in action throughout the rest of the North-West Europe campaign. He eventually became Chief of the General Staff, holding the post during the Falklands Campaign, and then Chief of the Defence Staff. He recently co-authored *The Chiefs* – the story of the United Kingdom Chiefs of Staff.

Air Marshal Sir Denis Crowley-Milling

A pre-war pilot in the RAFVR, Sir Denis flew in the Battle of France and the Battle of Britain in 1940 and later carried out fighter sweeps, bomber escort and fighter-bomber attacks over France, Belgium and Holland, flying both the Hurricane and the Spitfire. In 1943 he commanded a Typhoon ground attack wing in 83 Group and operated over northern France. Before and during the invasion period he was a member of the Combined Operations Planning Committee with the 8th USAAF.

On retirement in 1975 he became Controller of the RAF Benevolent Fund.

Lieutenant General Sir Napier Crookenden

Sir Napier was Brigade Major of 6th Airlanding Brigade, 6th Airborne Division. His Brigade landed in France on D-Day with the task of holding the southern perimeter of the Divisional bridgehead against 21 Panzer Division. He has written several books, including *Drop Zone Normandy*, a history of the 6th, 82nd and 101st Airborne Divisions in Normandy.

Dr Horst Boog

Dr Boog is a native of Leuna-Merseberg, where he suffered first-hand experience of allied bombing. In 1944, aged 16, he was trained as a glider pilot, and later transferred to the Volksturm. After the war, having spent a short time as a translator and interpreter at Nuremberg, he went to the USA as an exchange student, then worked for the USAF in Germany on intelligence duties. He studied part-time at the University of Heidelberg, obtaining his PhD in 1965. Since then he has worked in the Military History Research Office in Freiberg, first as Senior Air Historian and later as Chief Historian. He has lectured extensively inside and outside Germany, and has written several important works about the Second World War and the German Air Force.

Royal Air Force Historical Society

The Royal Air Force has been in existence for over 75 years; the study of its history is deepening, and continues to be the subject of published works of consequence. Fresh attention is being given to the strategic assumptions under which military air power was first created and which largely determined policy and operations in both World Wars, the inter-war period, and in the era of Cold War tension. Material dealing with post-war history is now becoming available for study under the 30-year rule. These studies are important to academic historians and to the present and future members of the RAF.

The RAF Historical Society was formed in 1986 to provide a focus for interest in the history of the RAF. It does so by providing a setting for lectures and seminars in which those interested in the history of the RAF have the opportunity to meet those who participated in the evolution and implementation of policy. The Society believes that these events make an important contribution to the permanent record.

The Society normally holds 3 lectures or seminars a year in London, with occasional events in other parts of the country. Transcripts of lectures and seminars are published in the Proceedings of the RAF Historical Society, which is a publication provided free of charge to members. Individual membership is open to all with an interest in RAF history, whether or not they were in the Service. Although the Society has the approval of the Air Force Board, it is entirely self-financing.

Membership of the Society costs £15 per annum and further details may be obtained from the Membership Secretary, Dr Jack Dunham, Silverhill House, Coombe, Wotton-under-Edge, Gloucester, GL12 7ND (Tel: 0453-843362).